AF623326

THE ADOLESCENT GIRL

Dr. Amrinder Bajaj
(Consultant Obstetrician & Gynaecologist
MBBS MD (AIIMS) Gold Medalist)

Books For All
Delhi-110052

Distributed by
D. K. Publishers Distributors Pvt. Ltd.
24, Ansari Road, Darya Ganj,
New Delhi-110 002
Ph: 327 8368, 326 1465, 327 8584
Fax : 326 4368
E-mail: dkpd@del3.vsnl.net.in
Web site: www.dkpd.com

First Published 2002
© Dr. Amrinder Bajaj
ISBN 81-7386-242-7

Published by
Books For All
(an imprint of Low Price Publications)
A-6, Nimri Commercial Centre,
Near Ashok Vihar Phase-IV, Delhi-110 052
Ph. : 740 1672, 745 2453
E-mail: lpp@nde.vsnl.net.in
Web site: www.lppindia.com

No part of this book may be reproduced, stored in or introduced into a retrieval system, or transmitted in any form or by any means (electronic, mechanical, photocopying, recording or otherwise), without the prior written permission of both the copyright owner and the above mentioned publisher of this book.
The views expressed here are those of the author and do not reflect the views of the Publisher.

Printed at
D. K. Fine Art Press Pvt. Ltd.
Delhi-110052 Ph. 745 2451

Printed in India

Dedicated

To

My mother who

Saw me smoothly

Through my adolescence

Author's note

Society and the medical profession have finally awakened to the special needs of the adolescent girl. The hormonal surge brings about drastic physical, mental and emotional changes that have to be dealt with in the right manner. With parents shying away from making their children sexually aware and sex education in schools yet in the infancy stage, an informative booklet would be of great help in educating this vulnerable section of society on reproductive health. It would also protect them from misinformation and its aftermath.

Contents

Part-1

Chapter

1.	The Adolescent Girl	9
2.	Anatomy Of The Female genital tract	15
3.	Menstruation	20
4.	Disorders In The Onset Of menstruation	24
5.	Menstrual Irregularities In The Adolescent	31

Part-2

6.	Premenstrual Syndrome	37
7.	Anemia In The Adolescent	43
8.	Hirsutism In The Adolescent	48
9.	Breast Diseases In The Adolescent	53

Part-3

10.	Adolescent Sexuality	58
11.	Adolescent Contraception	66
12.	Adolescent Abortions	74
13.	Adolescent pregnancy	71

Part-4

14. Vaginal Discharge & Sexually Transmitted Diseases (STD) 86
15. AIDS & The Adolescent 94
16. Pelvic Inflammatory Disease (PID) and Pelvic Tuberculosis 101
17. Vaginal Tampons & Toxic Shock Syndrome 108

Part-5

18. Mental health Of the Adolescent 110
19. Crimes Against The Adolescent Girls 117
20. Substance Abuse in the Adolescent 122

Part 1

Chapter-1

The Adolescent Girl

Society has finally awakened to the existence of the adolescent girl. It has begun to realise that adolescence is a period that needs special attention and care. Till a generation ago the bewildering changes that took place in a girl's life were kept under wraps. There were physical, emotional and psychological upheavals with which she was unable to cope. Menstruation came as a shock and was spoken of in hush-hush terms. The distraught girl was told was that she had become a woman now and had to be wary of predators called men. This confused her still further. She was not given a sex education simply because her mother did not receive any. Erratic, bizarre knowledge imparted by peers perplexed her still further.

The scenario today is equally dismal. The articulate, sophisticated, modern miss knows all or thinks that she knows all. "Information' pours out of TV, movies, commercials, pornography and all knowing friends. Parents today, are equally reluctant to talk about pubertal changes and the effect they have on the lives of their children. What is needed is a realistic, scientific approach to the seemingly unrealistic changes in a girl's life. Half-baked, half-truths from questionable sources will do her irreparable harm, hence this endeavour to put things in their right perspective.

What is adolescence?

There is no universally accepted definition of an adolescent. It can be loosely defined as a period of life when a carefree child becomes a responsible adult. WHO (World Health Organisation) defines adolescence as

* Progression from appearance of secondary sexual characters (puberty) to sexual and reproductive maturity.
* Development of adult mental process.
* Transition from total socioeconomic dependence to relative independence.

What is puberty?

Puberty is derived from the Latin word Pubertas, which means 'growing up'. It is that period of a girl's life, which stretches from the appearance of secondary sexual characters to the time she is able to undertake reproductive function. It is a major part of adolescence. The changes that take place are listed as follows: -

Physical feature	Age Range (in years)
Breast development	8-13
Hair in the genital region	9-13
Hair in the armpit	10-14
Height Gain	10-14
Onset of 1st menstruation	11-15 (mean 12.9)

Normal puberty starts by the age of 8-12 years in Indian girls and is completed in 3-4 years. At this stage girls usually look taller and older than boys of comparable age do because the onset of puberty occurs later in boys.

What factors affect the onset of Puberty?

The one major influence is genetic as seen by the concordance of the onset of menstruation in mothers and daughters, between sisters and women of the same ethnic group. Other factors like nutritional state, general health of the girl; geographical location, exposure to light and obesity also play a part. The age of menarche is usually earlier in children who are overweight.

Until which age can a person be called an adolescent?

Most reports include people between 10-20 years as adolescents while others cover those between 15-24 years. Adolescence can be further staged into

Stage 1 - between 12-14 years

Stage 2 - between 14-18 years

Stage 3 - nineteen and above.

Why does this period of life have a special importance?

Adolescents make up 15% of the population. Though they are the healthiest section of society there are a number of problems peculiar to this age group. The commonest amongst them are gynaecological problems like -

* Menstrual disorders.
* Vaginal discharge.

* Breast lumps.
* Obesity.
* Hirsutism.

Problems related to burgeoning sexuality -

* Sexually transmitted diseases including AIDS.
* Sexual abuse.
* Adolescent pregnancies and related health hazards.
* Unsafe abortions.
* Prostitution.

How do we address adolescent problems?

Adolescents are usually shy by nature and do not discuss their problems with the elders in their family. They are more likely to confide in a friend. A visit to the hospital is dreaded due to fear of discovery, long queues and indifferent, overworked, perfunctory staff. Talking with adolescents require special communication skills, hence the dire need of Adolescent Health Clinics where health personnel can interact with the teenager in an environment that is friendly, private and non-intimidating. The timings should be such that there is minimal disruption in educational or work schedules.

Teenagers should be encouraged to talk so that their fears and phobias, myths and confusions are cleared. Besides addressing the sexual and psychological aspects of adolescence a visit to the health clinic could be put to other uses too. This opportunity could be utilised to get their blood group tested and vaccinate them against Hepatitis B, varicella and MMR which have a direct bearing not only on the health of the girl but also her child bearing capacity. Infections like chicken pox, rubella and measles if contracted during pregnancy could lead to malformed babies. Vaccination at the time of adolescence ensures that such avoidable eventualities are prevented. The adolescent could also be examined physically and tested for tuberculosis and Sexually Transmitted Diseases (STD) including AIDS.

As Adolescent health clinics have yet to come up in a big way, what are the other ways by which we can address adolescent health problems?

It would be good if parents could tell their children what growing up is all about in a simple, sensible and scientific way. As most parents shy away from such a task, educational institutions form an ideal forum to tackle the matter. This could take the form of group discussions. A recently introduced, widely appreciated method is the 'Letter Box Approach'. Children are encouraged to put their queries in a letterbox over the week. These are opened by the teacher in front of the class on a particular day and answered one by one. As the same questions are often repeated, the teacher can begin with a simple lecture dealing with routine questions likely to be asked by an average teenager. After this the queries that have not been dealt with in the lecture can be tackled. Questions asked by adolescents of different stages vary.

Stage I adolescents studying in class 8th and 9th are inquisitive about the physical changes taking place in their bodies. They ask questions pertaining to menstruation, pregnancy and the physical appearance of the sexual organs of the opposite sex. It is a stage of getting used to the changes occurring in one's body.

Stage 2 adolescents (standard 10 and 12) though still preoccupied with menstruation and it's discomforts, express anxiety over their future reproductive lives. They are more concerned about the size of their body, their breasts, height and pimples. Sexual concerns are of paramount importance at this stage.

Stage 3 adolescents are usually college students. They are preoccupied with sexual intercourse, orgasm, masturbation, virginity and contraception and sexually contracted diseases.

This form of sexual education by a trusted and loved teacher is simple enough to be inculcated in the curriculum of every school. It is important that our adolescents are not left at the mercy of TV, blue films, pornography and ill informed peers to (dis) enlighten them. Let us lay a sound foundation for their future by making them physically capable, mentally strong, sexually secure and socially well-adjusted denizens of a bright new world.

Chapter-2
Anatomy of the Female Genital Tract

Before we embark upon the pleasures and travails of adolescence it will not be out of place to make our young readers conversant with the normal anatomy of the female genital tract. The mere mention of the subject was taboo till not so very long ago, but the knowledge about one's private parts, their functioning, care and hygiene is of paramount importance. Scientific information will go a long away in clearing the cobwebs of myths, erase unfound fears and save the woman and her sexual partner from embarrassment. There have been examples of couples coming for treatment of infertility with the wife's hymen intact! An ignorant pair blissfully indulged in anal intercourse and wondered why the wife did not conceive! A newly wed husband wanted to divorce his wife for being a 'eunuch'! Though she was tall, flat chested and bony she had normal sex organs. It is our endeavour to enlighten society so that such embarrassing situations do not arise.

The female genital tract can be divided into the external genitalia and the internal genital organs.

External Genitalia

The external genitalia of the female is called the vulva. The soft triangular area in front is the mons pubis. The mons splits lower down into thick, fleshy, vertical lips called the labia majora. At puberty, hair appears on the mons pubis and the external surface of the labia majora, while the internal surface remains hairless, pink and moist. Besides the sweat glands on the external genitalia (which produce a distinct odour characteristic of the female genitals) a pair of glands called the Bartholin's glands lies in the lower part of the labia majora with ducts opening just outside the hymen. These glands produce a lubricating mucous during sexual excitement.

The labia major enclose a pair of thin vertical pink inner lips called the labia minora that join anteriorly to enclose the clitoris. This corresponds to the penis in the male, becomes erect during sexual stimulation and plays an important part in female orgasm. The space within the labia minora is called the vestibule. This contains two openings. The smaller anterior urethral opening is for passing urine while the large one behind it is the vaginal orifice. This is the gateway to the internal genital system and is guarded by the much-hyped hymen - an object of many myths, debates and speculations. It is a thin membranous structure with a small eccentric opening that barely admits a fingertip in a virgin. It ruptures at first intercourse causing a variable amount of pain and bleeding. Occasionally the bleeding may be severe enough to require surgical intervention. At times the hymen may be so rigid that repeated attempt at coitus fail. An operative incision is needed to establish satisfactory sex. Rarely, it may be so elastic that it stretches and comes back to normal after intercourse. There have been prostitutes with an intact hymen! Besides intercourse, fall astride a sharp object, vaginal tampons and surgical procedures on the genital tract can lead to the rupture of the hymen without loss of virginity, though many girls are unnecessarily vicitmised on this account. On the other hand promiscuous girls mislead gullible husbands with the tale that the hymen ruptures at the time of menstruation. This is a falsehood because the hymen of a virgin has a hole large enough to allow menstrual blood flow.

The small area between the anus and the external genitalia is called the perineum. This comprises of muscles of the pelvic floor which support the pelvic organs. Trauma to this area particularly during labour can lead to the weakening of the support system and prolapse of the internal genital organs.

Internal Genitalia

The internal genitalia consist of a uterus (womb), a vagina and a pair of ovaries and fallopian tubes. The vagina is a longitudinal structure of about 4" with an elasticity that allows stretching during intercourse and delivery. Into the upper end of the vagina juts the cervix - the mouth of the uterus. During intercourse the semen is ejaculated high up in the vagina where is pools behind the cervix. The motile sperms swim upwards, through the cervical opening, into the uterus and beyond to fertilise the egg in the fallopian tube. The vaginal pH is acidic. A scanty amount of whitish secretion with a distinct odour is normal. Douching is an unnecessary, even harmful part of vaginal hygiene because it also removes protective bacteria exposing the vagina to attacks by harmful organisms.

It is sufficient to clean the external genitalia with a mild soap taking care to spread open the labia majora to wash the vestibular area. Strong soaps, detergents, deodorants and talcs should be avoided for they can cause allergic reactions. In fact talc had been found to be a predisposing factor for ovarian cancer! Underwear should preferably be of cotton and changed at least once a day. Nylons and tight underwear should be avoided.

The womb or the uterus is a pyriform structure measuring about 3 and half inches in length, 2 and half inches in width and 1 and a half inches thick. The bulk of the uterus is made of smooth muscles called the myometruim. The myometrium is covered externally by a thin shiny layer called the serosa and lined internally by the endometrium. The endometrium is prepared to a thick succulent state in the 1st 14 days of the menstrual cycle to receive the fertilised egg. If conception does not occur, it is shed along with the blood at the time of menstruation.

The ovaries are almond-shaped, pearly gray structures, situated on either side of the uterus. Besides producing the ova (eggs) they secrete female sex hormones which maintain the femininity of a woman and her pregnancy when it occurs. The ova are transported to the uterus by a pair of fallopian tubes. Each tube is 4" long. It arises from the upper lateral end of the uterus and opens over the ovary in the form of an inverted funnel. At this end are finger like structure called the fimbria that pick up the ova at the time of ovulation - around mid-cycle. The ovum is transported to the medial end of the tube by peristaltic movement of the tube. This is aided fine hair like structures called the cilia that line the interior of the tube and sweep the ovum forward. Fertilisation takes place in the tube. The fertilised ovum is pushed forwards by the same method of peristalsis and cilia and gets implanted in the uterus within 3-4 days of fertilisation.

The uterus and ovaries are held in place by various ligaments. The urinary bladder and urethra lies anterior to the uterus while the rectum and anal canal lies in close proximity posteriorly. A mention of these relations is important as quite often patients with genital problems may come with bladder and rectal symptoms and vice versa. Moreover difficult/traumatic deliveries and operation performed on the genital tract may injure the adjoining organs. As all these organs originate from the same mass of cells in intrauterine life, malformations of the genital organs may be accompanied by malformations of the urinary system and ano-rectal region.

Chapter-3
Normal Menstruation

The menstrual cycle of a woman has been steeped in mystery and myth since time immemorial. Most superstitions and beliefs associated with menses have been negative. This 'period' is considered 'unclean' and women are not allowed in kitchens and temples, even in modern India. In ancient times women were thought to be possessed by evil spirits and magical powers at the time of menstruation. The great Aristotle thought that the reflection of a menstruating woman could bewitch the next person who looked into the mirror! It is little wonder then that menstruation and related problems have been kept under wraps for ages.

What Is Menstruation?

Menstruation is the monthly flow of blood from the female genital tract. On an average the bleeding last for 3-5 days though anything between 2-8 days may be considered normal. The period between the 1st day of one period to the beginning of the next is called a menstrual cycle (MC). It is usually a 28 days cycle but a week this way or that is within normal range. The onset of menstruation at puberty is called menarche while its cessation in middle age is called menopause.

Why Does It Occut?

A complex hormone delivery system governs the sexual and reproductive functions of a woman. The hypothalamic pituitary axis situated in the brain produce hormones that induce the ovaries to produce sex hormones, which in turn act upon target organs like the uterus.

The pituitary produces FSH in the first half of the MC, which leads to the production of oestrogen in the ovary. This is responsible for the maturation of one ovum (of the lacs present in the ovary) in a fluid filled follicle. Under the influence of oestrogen the endometrium (inner lining of the uterus) becomes thick and succulent to receive the fertilised ovum.

Around the 14th day of the cycle there is a surge of pitutary hormone called the LH, which leads to the rupture of the follicle and the release of the ovum (ovulation) from the ovary. This is picked up by the tubal fimbria and transported through the tube towards the uterus. The ovary now produces progesterone in addition to oestrogen to continue the hectic preparation in the uterus - for the first ever nursery for the human baby. In case fertilisation does not take place in that cycle and there is no baby to nurture the uterus sheds 'tears of blood'. This 'weeping' or the menstrual flow is the culmination of the menstrual cycle. The thickened endometrium, which is of no use now, is shed along with the menstrual blood and the cycle is repeated in the next month and the next throughout the reproductive life of a woman.

Social Implications

The pubertal girl should be prepared well in advance for the advent of menses so that she is not taken unawares or misinformed by ignorant peers. She should inform her mother when she starts her periods so that she can be taught how to manage the blood flow. If at school she could report to a female teacher or the nurse/ doctor in the sick room. As reproductive maturity precedes mental maturity it is wise to warn her about the adverse effects of physical intimacy with the opposite sex.

Myths and beliefs implanted in the mind of an impressionable girl at the time of menarche have lifelong repercussions. Hence it is mandatory that menstruation be viewed in its right perspective - that of a normal physiological function. She should be taught menstrual hygiene and the right way of using and disposing pads. Stress should be laid on utmost cleanliness. Tampons are best avoided in virgins or used sparingly - keeping in mind a life threatening condition called 'toxic shock syndrome' that can occur as a result of tampon use. Bathing is not contraindicated; neither is moderate physical activity provided the girl does not have severe pain or excessive menstrual flow.

On no account should minor discomforts be amplified and the girl taught to resign herself to the 'curse' that is the lot of women to bear. Absenteeism from school should be discouraged unless her problem is severe enough to warrant medical intervention. She should be taught not to feel 'impure' as it diminishes her sense of self worth. Segregation from the rest of the family, separate food and utensils (as practiced in some parts of India) or avoidance of social activities is impractical and scientifically unnecessary. Menstruation should not be a hindrance for normal day-to-day activities. Abstaining from religious ceremonies depends entirely upon the orthodoxy of the family but hormone pills for postponement of periods on account of a religious pilgrimage or function are best avoided.

It is a wise mother who keeps a tab on the menstrual dates of her daughter for any woman between 12 to 45 who misses her periods should be considered pregnant unless proved otherwise. Though family values may be strong, peer pressure and media exposure usually get the better of the vulnerable girl stepping into adulthood. Though a large number of girls do tend to have erratic periods for some time after menarche. It is good to be over cautious and avoid complications later on.

Chapter-4
Disorders in the Onset of Menstruation

Normal puberty (sexual maturity) starts by the age of 8-12 years in Indian girls and is completed in 3-4 years. Menstruation is the culmination of the sexual development of a girl child. This is preceded by the development of breasts, gain in height and growth of axillary and pubic hair. Menarche - the first menstruation usually occurs between the ages of 11 to 15 years of life, the mean age being 12.9 years.

Not all girls are fortunate enough to go through the process of maturation in a normal manner. Things can go haywire at any level. She may start her periods before time or she may not start them at all. Her periods may be excessive or erratic. On the other hand they may be delayed or scanty. There may be severe pain during periods or she may develop masculine traits like hair growth and pimples.

Disorders in the onset of menstruation can be divided into - Amenorrhoea when a girl does not start menstruation by the age of 16 years and Precocious

Puberty when pubertal changes begin before the age of 8 years.

Amenorrhoea

Amenorrhoea can be primary - when a girl has never menstruated or secondary - when there is cessation of menstruation after menstruation has been established. A girl who hasn't developed breasts and sexual hair by 14 years of age or, a girl who has normal development of secondary sexual characters but has not started menstruating by the age of 16 years has to be evaluated thoroughly.

Shy on matters regarding her sexuality an adolescent girl is hesitant to discuss her problems with anyone. The clinic, the hospital atmosphere and a stern doctor usually intimidate her. Her overanxious mother on the other hand does all the talking. She is worried that her daughter's gynecological problems may mar her marital prospects. It is the doctor's duty to put both at ease. After allaying the mother's fears it is wise to talk to the girl separately. Dealing with a human being at this stage of life requires special communicative skills. It is imperative that her trust is won and the doctor is able to draw her out. A thorough history in a comforting atmosphere and a general physical examination of the girl should be done. Is her height and weight normal for her age group? What are her eating habits? Girls with extreme weight consciousness hardly eat anything, which results in an eating disorder called anorexia nervosa. This can also lead to amenorrhoea, which is cured once she resumes her normal eating habits.

Presence or absence of secondary sexual characters is specifically noted. Tuberculosis and thyroid dysfunction can also cause menstrual irregularities and have to be looked for. In cases of secondary amenorrhoea, however innocent the girl looks, pregnancy should be ruled out before proceeding with other investigations. Suggestion of a pregnancy test usually puts them on the defensive. Instead, an ultrasound can be suggested, which besides confirming or ruling out pregnancy gives other useful information.

Girls who have normally developed breasts, axillary and pubic hair and have not started menstruating usually have a normal functioning ovary (which supplies the hormones necessary for sexual maturation) but an abnormal passage. She may have the following

* Imperforate hymen.
* Absent vagina.
* Absent uterus.
* Absent uterus and vagina.

Imperforate Hymen

In cases of an imperforate hymen a girl menstruates regularly but there is no exit for the menstrual blood. As a result of this she suffers from cyclical pain in her lower abdomen around the time she normally should have had her periods. Due to the collection of blood in the genital tract a mass may be felt in the abdominal cavity. Examination of the external genitalia reveals a tense, bulging, and bluish membrane. All that the girl needs is an incision in the imperforate hymen for exit of the collected blood and for establishment of normal periods.

Absent Vagina

These cases are diagnosed by local examination, and ultrasound. They are relatively more difficult to treat as the reconstructed vagina has tendency to stenose (narrow) or even close down once again. In extreme case the blood filled uterus may have to be removed.

In the above mentioned cases menstrual blood may flow in a retrograde fashion and enter the abdominal cavity through the fimbrial end of the tube. Bits of endometrium that enter the abdomen with the blood have a tendency to implant on various organs of the abdominal cavity leading to menstruation within the abdomen every month! As the collected blood has no escape route it collects and coagulates inside the abdomen leading to agglutination of the ovary tubes and uterus forming painful pelvic masses. This condition is called endometriosis and needs prolonged hormonal treatment.

Absent Uterus

This is diagnosed by ultrasound and diagnostic laparoscopy. There is no treatment for this condition. The girl will never menstruate or conceive. The girl can either be marry person who already has children or if she is desirous of a child of her own, the eggs from her ovaries can be harvested, fertilized and put in the womb of a surrogate mother.

Absent Uterus And Vagina

This again is confirmed by ultrasound and diagnostic laparoscopy. As reproductive functions are nil, with an absent uterus (as stated above) the vagina can be reconstructed by plastic surgery for coital purposes prior to marriage.

An important point to be noted is that, as the urinary system grows together with the genital system defects in the womb. Defects in the genital system should alert the doctor about such a possibility and the urinary system should be thoroughly investigated for congenital defects.

Coming to cases of amenorrhoea without development of secondary sexual characters. This could be constitutional - a case of delayed puberty in which case the girl matures late though it should be kept in mind the puberty delayed beyond the age of 17 is less likely to be physiological.

She may have just streak ovaries, which are of no use whatsoever. Chromosomal analysis will reveal genetic defects. Occasionally startling revelations are made - the child may be of indeterminate sex or she may have a normal uterus and vagina and male gonads. These rudimentary testes are usually present in the abdominal cavity and have to be removed, as there are high chances of cancerous changes occurring in them. X ray skull, CAT scan and MRI and blood hormonal assays will reveal problems (including tumours and malfunction) higher up in the brain, which may or may not respond to therapy.

Precocious Puberty

Precocious puberty is a condition when a girl attains sexual maturity before the age of 8 years. Precocious puberty is five times commoner in girls than in boys. Though in 75% of cases the cause is not known - when the precocious puberty is labeled idiopathic - the diagnosis of idiopathic puberty is reached only by exclusion. A thorough general physical examination, blood tests, ultrasound and brain scans are necessary to rule out tumours of the brain, ovaries and adrenal glands. Girls who mature sexually before the age of 4 years are more likely to suffer from diseases while in those above 4 years of age the precocious development is usually idiopathic.

It has been observed that girls with obesity, long standing hypothyroidism have greater chances of sexual precocity. Injury to the skull may also hasten sexual maturity, which usually starts 1-2 months after the injury. In cases of adrenal tumours masculine characteristics like hirsutism and acne can also occur

Once the diagnosis of precocious puberty has been made, life-threatening conditions like brain tumours have to be ruled out. After this, treatment is aimed at arresting, if possible even causing regression of sexual characters. As maturity occurs in the true sense, there is very real threat of sexual abuse and pregnancy. If not controlled or reversed in time this will lead to stunted growth. Last but not the least the psychological impact of these changes in so young a child has to be looked into. Thankfully drugs are available that achieve the above goals and should be taken under strict medical vigilance till such time the child attains her full growth in height and she reaches the age group when normal puberty occurs. Help of a gynecologist, endocrinologist and a child psychologist can be taken simultaneously. The medicines are stopped when X rays reveal a bone age of 13 or so when normal menstruation ought to start. The girl begins to have normal pubertal changes 1-2 months after stopping the drugs after which she can grow up like any other normal teenager.

Chapter-5

Menstrual Irregularities in the Adolescent

More often than not menstruation is erratic in the first few years after puberty. A girl's periods may be delayed and scanty, they may be excessive and come before the stipulated period of one month. Quite often the periods are accompanied by severe pain or are preceded by a cluster of symptoms that are grouped under the heading of premenstrual tension. Minor disturbances in the menstrual cycle are to be treated only with reassurance for they resolve on their own with time. Problems severe enough to lead to absenteeism from school, to pallor and psychological disturbances need to be looked into and treated promptly.

Menstrual disorders can be grouped under the following headings:

Dysfunctional Uterine Bleeding (DUB)

Normal menstrual cycle has been defined as a mean blood flow of 4 days (with a variation of 2-3 days) at an interval of 28 days (+7 days). The amount of blood loss should be between 30-80 ml of blood. Therefore a menstrual cycle that lasts for more than seven days comes before 21 days and the loss of blood is more than 80 ml should be considered abnormal. This can be due to an organic cause like fibroids, polyps, and cancers of the genital tract, local injuries and foreign bodies in the vagina. Pregnancy complications and blood clotting defects should be ruled out. The most likely cause is hormonal disturbances when the condition is called DUB. Diagnosis of DUB is made only after the other causes for excessive menstruation have been ruled out.

Once DUB has been confirmed, the girl is treated according to her symptoms and the degree of her anemia, which is directly dependent on her menstrual blood loss. If the DUB is of the mild variety and her haemoglobin is more than 10gms % all that the girl needs is reassurance. She is told to take a proper diet, exercise and stress management. Iron and calcium pills help. She is asked to maintain a menstrual calendar and is reviewed after 6 months. This condition usually resolves itself with time.

Girls who have profuse, recurrent irregular cycles need hormonal therapy. There is a strong bias against hormonal treatment in young girls and their mothers oppose it vehemently. They fear that it will make the girl obese or worse still interfere with her future reproductive life. This is not the case. The very purpose of the initiation of the menstrual cycle is the induction of ovulation (production of the egg). Many young girls do not ovulate in the first few menstrual cycles due to the imbalance of the two major ovarian hormones estrogen and progesterone. Anovulation is the commonest cause of DUB in a young girl. Proper medication under strict medical supervision will regularise her cycles, decrease the blood loss, treat the anemia and improve her general health.

Rarely an adolescent girl suffers from such an acute episode of bleeding that her Hb falls to less than 7gms%. The girl may have to be hospitalised and given blood transfusions. Blood coagulation defects have to be specifically checked for. She has to be put on injectable hormones till such time her bleeding stops after which she can be switched on to oral pills.

Oligomenorrhoea

Oligomenorrhoea is the name given to scanty and delayed periods. It is usually due to infrequent ovulation (egg production), which is a common occurrence after menarche. It tends to right itself of its own accord after a year or so and does not need active treatment. Besides physiological reasons, conditions like TB, anorexia nervosa, excessive weight loss, emotional stress, hormonal disturbances due to pituitary, thyroid, adrenal and ovarian pathologies can cause oligomenorrhoea. However young the girl is pregnancy should be ruled out whenever there is a history of delayed periods.

Treatment is aimed at reassuring the girl and her family that the condition is self-limiting and needs no treatment. Also that, usually it does not affect future fertility. Those who have imposed severe diet restrictions upon themselves should be advised against it. In cases where a cause for oligomenorrhoea is found, treatment should be initiated accordingly.

Poly Cystic Ovarian Disease (PCOD)

A girl with PCOD is usually obese, has excessive hair growth with a masculine distribution, acne and periods that are delayed from I 1/2 to six months. Some girls menstruate only after taking medicines. To the triad of obesity, hirsutism and delayed periods is added infertility when she gets married. PCOD is known to run in families. It is a hormonal problem caused by excessive production androgens (male hormones) from the ovaries and adrenals. The menstrual irregularities are caused by chronic anovulation (absence of egg production) due to unopposed production of estrogen. Is this state of affairs is allowed to continue untreated to womanhood it predisposes the patient to uterine cancer. The excessive weight increases the risk of cardiovascular disease and diabetes in later life.

The girl is advised to lose weight not only for aesthetic purposes but also for therapeutic reasons. A myth amongst most Indian mothers is that the retention of menstrual blood in the body leads to obesity. In fact it is the other way round- loss of excess weight leads to resumption of normal periods. Moreover menstrual blood does not get retained in a girl with a normal passage. If weight loss does not give the desired results hormones (chiefly progesterone to counteract the unopposed production of estrogen) have to be given at regular intervals not only to right her menstrual cycles but also to stop further hair growth and prevent uterine cancer in later life. For hair that has erupted at places not becoming in a girl, electrolysis is the best bet.

Dysmenorrhoea

Dysmenorrhoea is defined as severe cramping pain in the lower abdomen occurring just before or during periods. It is a traumatic experience for the adolescent girl, converting a natural event into a period of pain. Dysmenorrhoea is further divided into primary and secondary dysmenorrhoea.

Dysmenorrhoea is called primary when no underlying pathology is responsible for the pain. It begins on the first day of menstruation and lasts for 12 - 24 hours. The pain is felt in the lower abdomen back and legs. Nausea, vomiting and headache may accompany it. The pain is severe enough in 5-10% of cases to make the girl miss school or college. It can lead to fear psychosis in the adolescent.

Secondary dysmenorrhoea begins before menstruation and lasts through the entire bleeding phase of the cycle. It is commoner in older women and is secondary to recognizable problems in the genital tract like uterine anomalies, endometriosis, pelvic inflammatory disease and tumours. Help of ultrasound, laparoscopy, and hysteroscopy is sought to diagnose the cause of painful periods. Treatment of the causative condition cures the dysmenorrhoea.

Primary dysmenorrhoea is the commoner of the two conditions, especially in the younger age group. Family history is present in 20% of cases. Diagnosis is confirmed only after ruling out pelvic pathologies. The girl needs reassurance that nothing is seriously wrong with her. She does not have to endure the pain, as it can be suppressed by medicines till the condition eventually rights itself. Painkillers are effective in 70% of the cases if given right at the beginning and continued at 4-6 hourly intervals. Girls who need contraception or those you do not respond painkillers can be put on oral contraceptives if the pain is debilitating enough to restrict activities.

In conclusion it is necessary to draw the attention of the adolescent girl to the fact that however problematic her case may seem - scanty, profuse, painful menses - most of the irregularities at this age are self-limiting and will go away with time. Meanwhile she should not endure her sufferings in stoic silence as 'the fate of womanhood'. There is treatment available for all the above and she should not hesitate to go to a doctor for the same.

Part- 2

Chapter-6

Premenstrual Syndrome

It was in the early twentieth century that Frank recognised as a cluster of symptoms that occur before menstruation and coined the term Premenstrual Syndrome (PMS). Though the condition can occur in any women of reproductive age it is not an uncommon affliction in the adolescent girl.

What is PMS?

PMS is defined as the cyclic recurrence of physical, psychological and behavioural symptoms that occur prior to menstruation and resolve after the onset of periods. As almost 75% of menstruating women suffer from discomfort in the pre-menstrual phase. As this is usually mild, it requires no treatment. Symptoms must be of sufficient severity to produce social, familial and occupational disruption; they should have occurred in at least 4 of the previous 6 cycles to be called PMS. Only 3-8% of menstruating women fall in this category.

What are the signs and symptoms of PMS?

These can be psychological and physical.

Psychological:

* Fatigue
* Irritability
* Anxiety
* Mood swings
* Depression
* Over-sensitivity
* Easily provoked to tears
* Anger
* Forgetfulness
* Food cravings
* Feeling of isolation.
* Poor concentration

Physical symptoms are: -

* Bloating
* Breast tenderness
* Headache
* Dizziness
* Hot flushes
* Palpitations
* Gastrointestinal symptoms
* Poor co-ordination

How is the diagnosis of PMS reached"?

A woman presenting with the above symptoms is examined thoroughly to rule out any medical, gynecological or psychiatric disorders. Many psychiatric disorders are known to worsen in the premenstrual phase. Detailed history, specifically of drug intake is taken. If no cause is found for her symptoms, she is asked to chart a 'Calendar of Premenstrual Experiences (COPE)' - for at least 3 cycles after her initial visit to the doctor. She is also asked to rate her symptoms daily on a scale of 0-3.

0 - indicates no symptoms.

1 - symptoms present but not severe enough to impair work.

2 - indicates symptoms interfering with work.

3 - indicates symptoms causing incapacitation; or requiring medical therapy.

PMS is confirmed: -

1. In the presence of at least one physical and one psychological symptom five days before the onset of menstruation in at least 3 consecutive cycles.
2. Relief of symptoms within 4 days of menstruation and relief maintained till at least day 12 of the menstrual cycle.
3. Symptoms are not due the side effects of drug intake.
4. There is marked social dysfunction in the form of marital discord, suicidal tendencies, neglect of children and poor work performance.

Are there any tests that can confirm or rule out the diagnosis of PMS?

No. There is no quantitative or investigative measure that can clinch the diagnosis of PMS.

What is the treatment of PMS?

This has to individualised depending upon the leading symptom. However there are certain general measures that have to be taken by women suffering from PMS. These include dietary changes, life style modification, stress management, vitamin and mineral supplements.

Dietary modifications include

* Reduced intake of salt, which decrease the water retention and bloating sensation.
* Small frequent complex carbohydrate meals.
* Reduce intake of chocolates, alcohol, tobacco and junk food in the second half of the cycle.
* Reduce intake of caffeine.
* Limit intake of animal fat.
* Regular meals.
* Weight reduction if obese.

Life style modification include

* 1-2 miles brisk walking at least 4-5 times a week.
* Stress reduction by meditation at least for 20 minutes a day.
* Interaction with close friends.
* Light reading or poem recitals are known to reduce negative mood patterns.
* Join a self-help group if available or read self-help books.

Vitamins and minerals

* Vitamin B6

* Vitamin E
* Vitamin A
* Evening primrose oil
* Zinc, copper. Calcium, magnesium etc. have all been tried with promising results in milder cases.

Any form of therapy has to be tried for at least 3 months to confirm whether it is effective or not. Treatment of physical symptoms has to be individualised.

* Mild diuretics in the premenstrual phase treats bloating. This acts by increasing the urine output and reducing the amount of water retained in the body.
* Good support, decreased caffeine intake, oral contraceptives and other drugs manage breast tenderness.
* Antidepressant drugs treat mood swings. These are to be taken under strict medical supervision.
* Premenstrual migraine, cramps and body aches are treated with appropriate painkillers.

Recent advances in treatment include exposure to bright artificial light at 7pm for 1/2 to 1 hour every evening and late night sleep deprivation. These have been tried (with promising results) to correct the presumed alteration in circadian rhythm.

The 'temperamental behavior' of a female on certain days of her periods is not to be laughed at or slotted under deriding terms like hysteria. Her symptoms are genuine and deserve a cure not ridicule for PMS in severe forms is a debilitating condition. It can reduce a woman to contemplating suicide.

On her part, the girl has to learn to relax, think positively, go in for regular physical exercise and ensure a good night's sleep. She should communicate freely with her family and not bottle up feelings. Also she shouldn't postpone pending jobs for the premenstrual period or take difficult decisions at that time of her cycle. Though PMS can be incapacitating, the diagnosis is simple and symptomatic therapy helps most cases. As the exact cause is not known further research is needed for definitive medical cure.

Chapter-7
Anemias in the Adolescent

The girl child is rarely welcome in an Indian household. She is at a disadvantage from the very beginning of intrauterine life. If she is not destroyed in the womb, she is killed at birth. If her parents are 'kind' enough to let her live, they do so reluctantly, condescendingly. While the son gets the choicest morsel she has to make do with leftovers, which leads to malnutrition. While he gets an education, she is trained for 'domesticity' by toiling from dawn to dusk. More often than not she has worm infestation as a result of working in unhygienic conditions with bare hand in the fields and cattle-shed. If this has not already caused anemia the slight cough she suffers from, which is passed off as 'bronchitis', could be tuberculosis ravaging her frail undernourished body. Then comes the onslaught of menstruation, which, even if normal depletes her iron reserves. If the anemia is severe she may even land up in cardiac failure.

On account of the above she crosses the threshold of childhood into adolescence in a chronically anemic state. Early marriage, childbirth in quick succession, abortions, poor nutrition and overwork add their mite to the dismal scenario prevalent in rural India.

Her urban counterpart fares slightly better on account of the higher socioeconomic status and lesser physical burden. Except for some emancipated families where there is no discrimination between the sexes, girls in cities too are treated as second-class citizens. They are given poorer food and less educational opportunities than their brothers. Incipient anemia becomes overt with cyclical blood loss during menstruation. If the quantity of blood and duration of flow increases, as is wont to in cases of puberty menorrhagia, the haemoglobin levels deteriorated rapidly.

What are the signs and symptoms of anemia?

The girl may be completely asymptomatic, especially if the anemia progresses slowly over a prolonged period of time and her body get used to the decreased haemoglobin levels. She may suffer from dizziness, breathless, fatigue, irritability and palpitation. She may feel weak and tire easily. She has an increased susceptibility to common infections as her body resistance has decreased. Cough with blood stained sputum points towards tuberculosis. Fever with chills and rigors, is an indicator of either malaria or urinary tract infection, though the latter will be accompanied by frequency of urination, burning and even passing of blood in urine. An anemic girl has a sallow look with a pale tongue and nails.

What are the causes of anemia?

These could be

* Bleeding: The commonest site of bleeding is the genital tract due to increased and prolonged menstrual flow. Other sites are - the gastrointestinal tract and the respiratory system. Blood loss could occur from bleeding gums, peptic ulcer, hookworms and piles. She could also cough out a lot of blood in her sputum in case she is tubercular.

* Defective generation of blood: This is usually when the nutrition is deficient in factors necessary for blood building that include iron, vitamins and minerals. If could also be due to defective formation in the bone marrow in cases of aplastic anemia, sickle cell anemia and leukemias, which are comparatively rare.

* Increased destruction: Malarial parasites cause the breakdown of red blood cells, which result in anemia.

* Infections like urinary tract infection, tuberculosis and worm infestations.

* Blood clotting defects.

How is a case of anemia diagnosed?

A history of deficient dietary intake, passing of worms in stools, chronic infection like TB, urinary tract infection, a repeated attack of malaria has to be elicited. One has to ascertain whether she suffers from piles or bleeding gums. Goiter - enlargement of the thyroid gland situated in front of the neck has also to be looked for. By far the most important cause of anemia in this age group is excessive blood loss during menstruation; hence a detailed menstrual history is very informative.

What are the investigations that should be carried out?

A complete haemogram is done to ascertain the degree and cause of anemia. Malaria is confirmed or ruled out by a blood smear. Urine examination will give an idea about the presence of urinary tract infection. X-ray chest will show the presence or absence of TB. Stool examination will ascertain the presence of worm infestations and blood in feaces. Thyroid function tests may have to be carried out to find out whether the girl suffers from hyper or hypo functioning of the thyroid gland, which may sometimes be the cause of increased blood loss during periods. Pregnancy has to be ascertained, as the demands of the fetus further aggravate anemia.

How is anemia of adolescence treated?

The mainstay of therapy is treating the cause and replacing the haemoglobin deficit. Malaria if diagnosed, has to be treated at the earliest to prevent further deterioration in haemoglobin levels. Ova and cysts are eradicated from the gastrointestinal tract by thoroughly de-worming the girl. Urinary tract infection if present has to be treated with appropriate antibiotics. Tuberculosis needs prolonged treatment to effect a total cure. Piles and bleeding gums that cause a slow constant leak of blood have to be dealt with.

Puberty menorrhagia - excessive bleeding during periods in an adolescent girl, is by far the commonest cause of anemia at this age group. An ultrasound will show an occasional uterine or ovarian tumour that needs surgical treatment. If DUB is the cause, the blood loss is stemmed by hormone therapy. The menorrhagia usually corrects itself after 3-6 months of cyclical hormonal therapy. If it persists for prolonged periods bleeding disorders and clotting defects have to be looked into.

Besides treating the causative factor, the general health of the girl has to be improved. She could take a nutritious well balanced diet rich in proteins, green vegetables and fruits. Iron and other blood building factors like vitamin B and folic acid have to be supplemented in oral or injectible forms depending upon the severity of the anemia.

If the anemia is severe enough to cause congestive cardiac failure the girl has to be hospitalised and treated as an indoor patient till she comes out of the cardiac failure. Blood transfusion may also be required in extreme cases.

Anemia in the adolescent girl is a totally avoidable but yet rampant having far reaching consequences. It must be remembered that this young woman will one day become the pivot around which a new family unit revolves. Future generations of mankind will emerge from her womb. As with any structure, the foundation has to be strong enough to carry the entire edifice. It is the moral duty of parents to see to it that no teenage girl enters into adulthood with a heamogloblin deficit.

Chapter-8
Hirsutism & the Adolescent

For a burgeoning girl woman acutely aware of her newfound identity, growth of hair in areas other than normal is horrifying. Yet there are certain girls who suffer from disfigurement and intense mental torture on this account. This condition is called hirsutism.

Human hair can be divided into 3 categories depending upon its texture.

1. Lanugo - Very fine hair found in the fetal state. This can grow due to the intake of certain drugs such as Dilatin used for epilepsy.
2. Vellus Hair - Soft downy hair normally found at puberty.
3. Terminal hair - Coarse adult hair.

What is Hirsutism?

Hirsuitism is growth of hair in androgen sensitive areas i.e. areas normally under the influence of male hormones like the upper lip, chin and chest.

What is Virilism?

Virilism is the process of masculinisation carried

a step further with loss feminine contour, hoarseness of voice, baldness and enlarged clitoris.

Why does a girl have hirsutism?

There are three hormones circulating in a woman's body. Predominant are the feminine hormones - estrogen and progesterone. A small amount of the male hormone testosterone is also secreted by the ovary and the adrenals and is responsible for female libido. While progesterone has no effect on hair growth, estrogen decreases hair growth and testosterone, if produced in excess leads to hirsutism.

What leads to an increase in male hormones in a female body?

1. *Polycystic ovarian disease* (PCOD) can cause hirsutism. This condition is characterised by obesity, irregular or absent periods, hirsutism and infertility. These girls are more prone to diabetes and cardiovascular diseases later and have to be investigated for the same. When the onset of hair growth is abrupt and the progress rapid an ovarian tumour is to be suspected and the girl investigated accordingly.

2. *Adrenals* - these are endocrine glands situated on the top of the kidneys. Besides a host of other hormones they secrete a small amount of male sex hormone. When the functioning of the adrenals goes haywire or there is a tumour of the adrenal gland, hirsutism is one of the clinical manifestations.

3. *Drugs* - Certain drugs like Dilantin, Danazol, progestogens and anabolic steroids can also lead to hirsutism.

4. *Idiopathic* - When the girl is not on drugs; when she is of normal weight and has normal periods, when there is no malfunction of the ovaries and adrenals; in short, when no cause is found for hirsutism it is called idiopathic.

How does one diagnose hirsutism?

A detailed history of the time of onset and the rapidity of progress has to be taken. Associated factors like menstrual irregularities and obesity have to be looked for. Depending upon the amount of hair at a particular place it is graded between 1-4. Presence of hair at the following sites is considered abnormal.

1. Upper lip
2. Chin
3. Chest
4. Back
5. Lower abdomen
6. Upper abdomen
7. Lower thigh
8. Upper thigh
9. Buttocks

Excessive growth of hair on the forearms and legs is not included in hirsutism.

How is a girl with hirsutism to be investigated?

Once the disease has been diagnosed and graded we proceed with the investigations. The amount of circulating male hormones in the blood is estimated. Certain blood tests tell us about the source of these hormones - the ovaries or the adrenals. This is important as treatment varies accordingly. Thyroid function tests have to be done to rule out hypothyroidism. Ultrasound is helpful in diagnosing PCOD. Once confirmed, blood sugars and lipid profile of the girl have to be done, as abnormalities of the same are usually associated with PCOD. If the onset of hirsutism is abrupt and the progress rapid an ovarian or adrenal tumour is to be suspected. This can be confirmed or ruled out by a CAT scan.

How is hirsutism to be treated?

The goal of the treatment is to remove existing hair and prevent further hirsutism. If the cause is found, be it PCOD, hypothyroidism, tumours the underlying disease is treated. If the girl is on drugs that lead to abnormal hair growth stop them. If they are essential for her treatment replace them with drugs with lesser side effects.

The unwanted hair causes psychological havoc and has to be removed at the earliest. There are certain drugs that suppress or block the action of androgens on the skin. This arrests further hair growth and even leads to the regression of hair already present. One has to take them for at least 3 months to learn whether they are effective in a particular case or not. Even if the only change seen at the end of 3 months is the change in texture of the hair from terminal hair to vellus hair it is a positive sign. Continuation of treatment will lead to eventual disappearance of unwanted hair.

There is a much-touted myth amongst the lay public that hair removed by shaving or waxing grows again with a vengeance. This is not true. Mechanical methods of Hair Removal do not worsen Hair Growth. Electrolysis is a good and permanent method for removing unwanted hair for those who can afford it.

In conclusion I would like to state that though hirsutism is a distressing symptom it is treatable. Under the expert guidance of a gynecologist, endocrinologist and beautician, there is no reason why any girl should suffer from unwanted hair.

Chapter-9
Breast Diseases in the Adolescent

Of the various changes that take place during adolescence, breast development is the most visible sign of sexual maturity and hence of great import to the growing girl. Anything other than normal - be it early or late development, extra large or small breasts embarrass her. As there is a wide variation in the onset and progress of thelarche (breast maturation) in different individuals, these discrepancies can be mistaken for abnormalities leading to untold anguish and even uncalled for biopsies at times! This usually occurs when one breast develops faster than the other breast and the breast bud is mistaken for a lump. Lumps are rarely present in the pre-pubertal breast but if they do occur malignancy must be kept in mind.

Abnormalities of breast development that can occur at this phase of life are:

* *Failure of breast development*: This is usually due to a defect called Turner's Syndrome, where chromosomal analysis reveals that the girl has neither XX (female

configuration of sex chromosomes) nor XY (male) chromosomes but XO. Besides absence of breast development virilisation can occur due to abnormal functioning of the adrenal glands. Very rarely do girls with normal menstruation have absent breasts though rudimentary breasts do develop later on. If the absence of breasts affects the girl psychologically she can be offered reconstructive surgery after she has attained adulthood.

* *Precocious Development*: When breast development and other pubertal changes occur before the age of 8 years it is called precocious puberty. This could be idiopathic, when no cause is found or due reasons as varied as life threatening brain tumours, injury to skull and hypothroidism. If a cause is found treatment of the cause takes precedence. If no cause is found drugs to arrest further breast development and/or cause regression of breast and periods can be given till the girl reaches the appropriate age of menarche.

* *Adolescent hypertrophy*: There may be abnormal enlargement of either or both breasts leading to embarrassment, anxiety and discomfort. There may be unilateral or bilateral neck and shoulder pain due to the additional weight borne by the spine. Reduction mammoplasty (decrease in size of the breast) by plastic surgery may be needed in some girls for cosmetic reasons and to reduce the strain on the spine.

* *Nipple discharge*: This could be physiological in a rapidly growing breast and is associated with menstruation. It may occur in girls on oral contraceptive

pills or breasts that are subjected to repeated nipple stimulation. Other causes of nipple discharge could be brain tumours, increase in level of Prolactin hormone and hypothyroidism. The discharge disappears on treating the cause. A blood stained discharge in a young girl could be due to papilloma in the milk ducts. Treatment consists of surgical excision of the duct containing the papilloma.

* *Benign Breast disease*: This is the commonest breast related problem and can occur at any age of reproductive life though the adolescent girl is acutely aware of such an occurrence and reports earlier. It is characterised by unilateral or bilateral breast pain, which may or may not be cyclical. If cyclical it usually starts a few days before menstruation and disappears of its own accord after the onset of periods. There may be mild tenderness to excruciating pain though on examination no well-defined mass is found. Treatment in both cyclical and non-cyclical variety consists of reassurance, good breast support, painkillers, Vitamin E or GLA 120. Severe cases may require drugs like Danazol, which have to be given under strict medical supervision.

* *Fat necrosis*: This can occur in any age group and is usually the result of repeated trauma. The fibrosis of the breast tissue that occurs after fat necrosis leads to abnormality in the shape of the breast and discrepancy in the appearance of both breasts leading to a suspicion of cancer. Cancer of the breast is an extremely rare occurrence in the adolescent.

* *Breast Lumps*: The commonest form of breast lump in a young girl is fibro-adenoma. This is a non-cancerous firm, non-tender, mobile mass in the breast. It is also called the 'breast mouse' on account of its mobility. It can be single or multiple, can occur in either or both the breast and can very in size from a small nodule to very large masses. The standard treatment is removal of the mass, especially if very large. If small and multiple and filling both breasts they can be carefully monitored with ultrasound and fine needle aspiration biopsy (FNAC). The girl should be called for regular follow-ups. Mammography - multiple X Rays of the soft tissue of the breast - may also be required

It would not be out of place here to teach an adolescent girl the art of self-examination of the breast. This will stand her in good stead throughout her adulthood life, when far more serious breast complications are likely to occur. Self-examination of the breast leads to the early discovery of masses, discharge and disfigurement making them more amenable to treatment.

Self-examination of the breast should be carried out at least once a month, preferably after the periods. The girl should sit or stand in front of the mirror with the upper part of her body bare. After looking critically for any physical abnormalities in both breasts and nipples (slight variation in size and position of the breasts can be taken as normal) she should raise her hand upwards and again observe for any discrepancy.

After this she should lie down on her back with a pillow under her head. A small pillow or a folded towel is placed under her right shoulder. The right hand is put under the head. The left hand is used to palpate the right breast and vice versa. The breast is divided into four imaginary quadrants and the palpation begun from the upper inner quadrant from the outside towards the nipple by making small circular motions with the flat of the fingers and *not their tips.* The normal lobular fatty tissue of the breast may appear lumpy if felt by the tip of the fingers or if grasped between thumb and four fingers. This may give rise to trepidation for entirely false reasons. The lower inner quadrant is also felt in the same way for lumps and nodules. To palpate the two outer quadrants the hand is removed from under the head and placed alongside the body. The procedure is repeated on the left side. The armpit on both sides is examined thoroughly in a similar manner as a part of the breast tissue called the axillary tail extends into this area as well. Last of all the nipple should be squeezed to look for any discharge, be it milk, pus or blood. If any abnormality is found it is prudent to report to the doctor immediately. More often than not reassurance will be all she needs, as most abnormalities in this age group are not life- threatening.

Part- 3

Chapter-10

Adolescent Sexuality

Adolescence is a period of sexual maturity. There is a surge for female sex hormones that alter the physical contours of a child into that of a woman. There is maturation of internal and external genitalia and growth of secondary sexual characters in preparation for a fulfilling reproductive life. As sexuality is a pre-requisite to reproduction there are psychosexual changes of a magnitude hitherto unknown. A bewildering new array of emotions assails her. She is excited and apprehensive, thrilled and terrified, liberated and confined at the same time. Unsure of herself, she moves two steps forward and one step backwards. She becomes aware of her newfound sexuality welcoming it at times and resenting it at times. She is proud yet shy of her burgeoning breasts her rounded hips and the pleasurable sensations that course through her body. She becomes aware of the power she has over the opposite sex and revels in it. Quite often she is unable to cope with the havoc caused by surging hormones leading to disastrous results.

The paradox of adolescence is that sexual maturity precedes mental maturity. As a result she is confused and erratic in her behaviour. She is rebellious and rude and does not like to abide by rules. She tries to assert her independence and resents parental authority. Peers take precedence over seers and whatever her friends do is right no matter what her seniors say to the contrary. She takes an inordinate interest in her appearance and tries to make herself attractive to the members of the opposite sex. It is the most vulnerable period of her life when she can easily fall into the trap of drugs and sexual abuse. In the competitive world of today it is also the time she has to choose her career. The stress of preparing for an adult life makes many a youngster buckle under the strain.

What factors influence teenage sexual behavior?

The sexual behaviour of an adolescent is influenced by various factors such as education, social strata, ethnic norms and family background. Religious influences, peer pressure, interpersonal relationships, mass media, social values, culture and tradition. Sex education or the lack of it also plays a vital role. Girls in Indian villages have early sex due to early marriage. Street children indulge in 'survival sex' where they trade sex for food, money, protection or drugs.

How do adolescents deal with their sexuality?

There are but 3 options open to the adolescent.

1. Early marriage
2. Premarital sex
3. Abstinence

Early Marriage

Teenage marriage is the social custom in India especially in states like Rajasthan, Bihar, MP and UP - the mean age of marriage being 17 years. Though it contains the adolescent sexuality within the limits of social sanction, though it prevents premarital sex and the attending repercussions of unwed mothers, illegal abortions, prostitution and sexually transmitted diseases there is much to be said against it. For one it restricts the socioeconomic development of the girl (as most are unable to complete school or get vocational training of any sort) and limits her role to that of child bearing and child rearing. As most are unaware of contraception even legitimate pregnancies at this age pose a problem. Complications like anemia, pregnancy-induced hypertension (PIH), small pelvis, immature perineum, premature babies are common in mothers of this age group leading to a higher incidence of fetal and maternal deaths.

Premarital Sex

People tend to believe that with the onslaught of media titillation, exposure to western culture, easy access to pornographic literature premarital sex is on the rise. Though the modern miss is more blatant this observation is not entirely true. Ancient Indian women dressed as provocatively as girls of today. Centuries ago Aristotle observed, "Of all bodily desires, it is the sexual one to which adolescents are most disposed to give way and in regard to sexual desire they exercise no restrain." It is the responsibility of society to inculcate the principles of reproductive health in adolescence. The fall out of inadequate sexual education is mind-boggling. Premarital sexual activity puts the adolescent to grave risk. 15 million girls between the age of 15-19 years give birth and 4 million under go abortion each year. A 100 million are infected with sexually transmitted diseases and 40% of all new HIV infections occur amongst the 15-24 years olds, ruining their lives irrevocably. Approximately 20% of sex workers are adolescent girls. In Thailand of the 800,000 prostitutes who are under the age of 20, 200,000 are less than 14 years! Early age of coitus and multiple sex partners also increase a woman's susceptibility to cancer of the cervix.

Problems arise when adolescents do not have access to proper information as regards sexual health. Most pitfalls of growing up can be avoided by good counseling. With the early onset of puberty and delayed marriages in urban society there occurs a prolonged gap between sexual maturation and socio-legal consent to sexual activity. This leads to premarital sex in an increasing number of teenagers. Most of them indulge in sex out of curiosity or because their friends profess to be doing it. Heightened libido at this age and the intense pleasure obtained by sexual union drives many a teenager to premarital sex. In a survey of unmarried pregnant girls conducted at a general hospital that catered to the lower socioeconomic strata it was found that rape occurred in only a small percentage of cases. Most girls entered a physical relationship willfully for reasons that included promise of marriage, receipt of gifts and monetary benefits, at the insistence of boy friends or seduction by older male relatives. Most of them were not aware of contraception or repercussions in the form of disease and pregnancy.

Abstinece and Delayed Marriage

Though our country is trying to raise the age of marriage it has not succeeded very well so far. Abstinence is a declining practice all over the world. Those who do refrain from sexual intercourse often indulge in masturbation and end up feeling guilty for the same. There are so many myths surrounding masturbation and orgasm during sleep (nightfall in boys) that the teenager ends up feeling miserable. It should be impressed upon their minds that masturbation is neither harmful nor shameful. In fact it is the safest way of sexual release in our AIDS ridden times.

What is the role of society in managing psychosexual problems in adolescents?

This can be divided into

1. Parental responsibility:

It is not wise to be either too lenient or dominant. Strike a median course. Ask yourself what sort of behaviour will be detrimental to your child. Once you are convinced that certain activities are a definite no-no, assert your authority firmly and stick to it. Do not give in under the pressure of continuous pleading and whining of your wily adolescent. The adolescent tries to curry favour with the weaker parent so it is imperative that both parents put up a united front. Parents should invite her friends' home so that they learn what sort of company she keeps. They should be aware of they way she is spending her leisure time, with whom and how? See to it that she does not get hooked on drugs or enters the call girl racket to earn easy money for the good things in life. Be wary of expensive clothes and jewelry her friends seem to be giving her ever so often. Also keep a record of her last menstrual date.

2. Role of society:

Though she may be a cross between an adult and a child, though she may be going through an identity crisis, society should recognise the adolescent as a person and treat her as such. People at home college or place of work should ask her opinion, listen to her point of view and be amenable to reasonable demands. This will help her to grow as a human being and build her confidence. As rural girls are married soon after primary school, it is best to delay such marriages by giving them vocational training like sewing, basket weaving so that they are self sufficient and capable of holding their own in society.

3. Role of government:

The government should provide for total reproductive health care of the adolescent. This includes strict implementation of marriage age, centres for counseling with easy access to friendly gynecologists, social workers and psychologists. Facilities for safe abortion should be provided. Clinics and literature that make them aware of safe sex, sexually transmitted diseases and contraception should be within their reach.

Also condoms and other contraceptive devices should be made available to them at centres that do not look upon their need for contraception and safe sex with censure and disapproval.

4. Role of media:

Mass media especially TV has become the chief source of sex education for growing adults. As they have the power to shape the thinking of a whole new generation, they have a grave responsibility towards their gullible audience. It is up to them to correct the way they depict sex on screen. Real heroes have become harder to come by in modern times. More often than not film stars and TV personalities serve as role models and they should keep this in mind when they flaunt their lifestyles.

5. Sex education in schools:

Indian society is divided in this regard. Puritans state that it will encourage libertine behaviour in adolescents. Those for it say that the risks of no information or worse still inaccurate information far outweigh those of right knowledge given at the right time. Adolescents should be taught anatomy and physiology of the reproductive system, genital hygiene especially during periods, the advantages of delayed sexual activity, risks of unsafe sex, sex with multiple partners, teenage pregnancies and illegal abortions. They should be taught about contraception and the risk of venereal diseases and AIDS.

To sum up an adolescent is a confused person who, despite her aggressive and abrasive demeanor needs the support of family and society. In fact she needs it more now than ever before. Don't let her weird hairstyle; rude remarks and slang spouting prolonged telephonic conversations daunt you. Underneath she is still a frightened little girl trying to cover her fear by bravado. Make an effort to keep a good rapport with her and let her know that though she is allowed to cautiously try her wings she should feel free to come to you in times of trouble. Give her free rein to develop her personality but do not hesitate to tighten your hold when the need arises.

Chapter-11
Adolescent Contraception

Let me make it clear at the very outset that this article is not written to encourage promiscuity in the adolescent. As far as possible it is best to refrain from premarital sex for there is a host of physical, emotional and social problems associated with such indulgence. Physically there is always the risk of pregnancy, which, can further lead to unsafe abortion, or the horrifying prospect of being an unwed mother. A girl below the age of 16 has a greater chance of being affected with sexually transmitted diseases (STD) including the dreaded AIDS because of the immature genital system. Besides this they can suffer from pelvic inflammatory disease (PID) characterised by chronic pain in the lower abdomen, pain during intercourse (dyspareunia) and unhealthy discharge per vaginum. PID can further lead to blocked tubes, infertility and ectopic pregnancy - a life threatening condition when the pregnancy occurs in the tube instead of the uterus.

Emotionally the girl can be wrecked in a number of ways. She may be ditched by the very boyfriend she gave in to for being a girl of 'loose morals', this when he insisted that she sleep with him to prove her love for him! Besides the physical trauma, an abortion or a delivery can scar her psychologically for life. And if she fails to conceive after marriage due to a STD or PID, her cup of woe is full.

Socially she may be ostracised. Chances of making a good marriage are thwarted - if her premarital sexual activities and/or pregnancy become publicly known. Those who cross this hurdle get married only to face the next. If her husband discovers that she is not a virgin, marital discord and even divorce can follow. Yet again as a consequence of premarital sex if she proves to 'barren' chances of a normal married life are further jeopardised. In certain cases a sexual relationship before marriage may be but the beginning of a downslide to a life of prostitution.

As one can see, endless is the list of woes that can befall a girl if she if she indulges in promiscuous behaviour. Why then this alarmingly increasing trend of premarital sex?

* With the decreasing age of puberty and increasing age of marriage in the urban population, years when sexual activity is at its prime are spent in the unmarried state. More often than not, the hormonal surge overcomes mental restrain leading to sexual indulgence.

* Nuclear families with working parents lack of vigilance, dwindling moral values, decreasing religious

pressures add to the licentious atmosphere.

* Peer pressure, media exposure, emulation of Western customs of dating, drug abuse etc.

* Being continually thrown against each other at educational institutes and place of work gives boys and girls ample space and opportunity to give vent to their sexuality.

* The unfortunate minority that has been subjected to rape or repeated sexual abuse by known and trusted adults.

* Call girls and prostitution racket. Touts lure young girls from far-flung areas with promises of jobs in big cities where they are sold to brothel owners. Supervisors coerce girls working in factories to submit to their advances. Most give in lest they lose their jobs. Then there are college girls who are not averse to making easy money on the side for the good things in life - for which their pocket money falls woefully short.

* Quite often sex is unplanned and takes place on the spur of the moment without knowledge of contraceptive measures or non-availability of the same.

* Last but not the least most of them have no inkling of the hazards of such a preoccupation.

For the above-mentioned reasons and the fact that a large number of teenagers in rural India are married, knowledge of adolescent contraceptive has become relevant. Unprotected intercourse amongst adolescents is chiefly due to limited access to family planning information. Unmarried adolescents find it difficult to obtain family planning services as these programs are targeted towards married couples. Social, religious, cultural and legal pressures further deny them the contraceptive protection they are in dire need of. Society should provide health care services including contraception for the sexually active youth. In fact a person at this stage of life will be more effectively motivated to use contraceptives.

What is the ideal contraceptive for the adolescent?

An ideal contraceptive for an adolescent should be 100% effective, safe with no side effects and have quick reversibility to fertility after stoppage of use. It should be easy to use, cheap and freely available. Unfortunately such a contraceptive does not exist. Nevertheless there is a variety to choose from. Contraceptive methods should be individualised keeping in mind their socioeconomic, educational, cultural and marital status. Devices available to the teenager are-

Barrier Methods

These include condoms, diaphragms, creams, foams, jellies and vaginal sponges. Besides contraception they protect the user from sexually transmitted diseases, including AIDS. They also reduce the incidence of pelvic inflammatory disease thus preserving the future fertility of the girl. The safest method of contraceptive for the teenager indulging in occasional sex is the condom. It is the most commonly used barrier contraceptive and has been around for years. It is easily available and cheap. It prevents both pregnancy and infections. It has no long-term derogatory effects on fertility. The disadvantages include high failure rate, interruption of coitus and interference with the pleasure of the act.

There are spermicidal creams and jellies that can be inserted in the vagina to kill the sperms. Vaginal tablets that put up a barrier of spermicidal foam also serve the same purpose. If creams and jellies are used along with the condom contraceptive efficacy is increased manifold. Disposable vaginal sponges moistened with two tablespoons of water can be inserted deep into the vagina 2 hours before coitus and removed 6 hours later. They act by preventing entry of the sperms into the cervix, absorbing the seminal fluid and killing the sperms. If forgotten inside it can lead to itching, malodorous discharge and infection.

Oral Pills

These are the most widely used method of contraception amongst the youth of the West. This is because they are simple to take, extremely effective and independent of the act of coitus. Besides they alleviate a host other problems known to occur in the adolescent girl. These include menstrual irregularities, premenstrual tension and menstrual cramps. To be effective they have to be taken regularly in the prescribed manner. As teenagers are forgetful more often than not an occasional missed pill can decrease the efficacy and also cause intermittent bleeding. There is also some degree of weight gain. This scares off quite a number of girls putting this highly useful method into disrepute. In India it has found favour with the educated teenager though the low literacy rate in rural areas has lead to poor compliance.

Emergency Contraceptions

This is ideal for unplanned occasional intercourse and for rape victims. All adolescents should be aware that such an option exists so that the agonsing suspense over the arrival of the next period need no longer be suffered. High dose oral pills can be taken within 72 hours of exposure. Pills like Ovral can be taken in the following manner - 2 tablets soon after the act and 2 tablets after 12 hours. This reduces the number of pregnancies by at least 84%. High dose of hormones can lead to nausea and vomiting and anti-emetics may have to be taken simultaneously.

Intra Uterine Contraceptive Devices (IUCD)

IUCDs like copper T are generally unsuitable for the teenage population. A foreign body lying in the uterus predisposes to genital tract infection and may lead to infertility due to blocked tubes. It is only to be considered in a recently delivered or aborted married teenager as a method of spacing. The advantage is that it has to be inserted only once to give contraceptive protection for at least 3 years. The disadvantages are - it needs medical personnel for insertion, can lead to excessive bleeding and pain during menstruation and increases the risk of pelvic infections. In exceptional cases it can also be used as an emergency contraceptive measure, especially if the girl reports later than 72 hours after coitus and the high dose contraceptive pill is of no use.

Miscellaneous

Under this heading can be included abstinence, safe period, coitus interruptus, masturbation and non-coital sexual activity. As mentioned earlier though abstinence is advisable it is not always possible amongst teenagers when the libido is at its peak. If they are wary of other forms of contraception adolescents can be taught some natural methods of preventing pregnancy. The time of the menstruation cycle when a girl is least likely to get pregnant is a few days before and after her periods. As ovulation takes place only once in a month, approximately at mid-cycle it is best to avoid intercourse during this unsafe period. Though not a foolproof method (particularly in girls with irregular periods) it can be tried. Coitus interruptus is when the male partner ejaculates outside thus preventing the deposition of semen inside the vagina. Masturbation and non-coital sexual activity are other alternatives to intercourse that satiate sexual desire without causing pregnancy.

Instead of hiding our heads like ostriches in the sand we should accept the fact that premarital sex has become a part of our social milieu. Though every attempt should be made to prevent or delay sexual activity in the teenager, it is best to deal with it in a sensible manner. There should be an open, improved parent child communication. They should help adolescents to resist pressure to become sexually active. Dating, if at all should take place in groups so that lesser opportunities are available to individual couples to indulge in sexual activities. At dates girls should be encouraged to pay for there own meals and cinema tickets so that they do not feel obliged to pay in a different kind of currency. The importance of sex education in school and colleges cannot be underestimated. Community and health care workers should make information regarding sex, contraception and pregnancy easily available to the young population. They should have easy access to contraceptive measures so that they do not fall prey to dreaded diseases and unwanted pregnancies.

Chapter-12
Adolescent Abortions

In 1971 the Indian government passed the Medical Termination of Pregnancy Act. This was done in order to cut down the number of illegal abortions performed and reduce the complications and deaths that resulted from such procedures. Though the married urban woman benefited vastly from this act the rural poor and unmarried females still went to untrained personnel for abortions. Paradoxically more illegal abortions were taking place in 1990 than at the time of passing the legislation. In fact back-street abortions outnumber legal MTP by a ratio of 11:1. Global studies indicate that of the 15 million illegal abortions performed worldwide, 4 million, the highest for any country, take place in India. Of these 20,000 Indian women die annually which is a shame for such deaths are entirely preventable. Despite the risks of debility and death, illegitimate pregnancies are on the rise. The reasons could be:

* Changing social values

* Increased discrepancy between the age of sexual maturation and marriage
* Long engagements
* Curiosity
* Contraceptive failure
* Sexual abuse/assault
* Socioeconomic pressures

Once an unwed teenager discovers that she is pregnant she options available to her are limited.

1. She could marry her partner in 'crime', which is not always feasible, as he may be unwilling, absconding, already married or even a close relative! Even where a marriage under duress is possible it is not always successful for the reasons are all wrong and there is a high rate of divorce.
2. She could continue with the pregnancy and become a source of disgrace and dishonour to her family. More often that not society and family disown her, she receives no physical care and emotional support, undergoes the travails and complications of a teenage pregnancy to produce an unwanted off spring who remains the butt of social cruelty all his life.
3. She could deliver and abandon the child or give it away in adoption to infertile couples or orphanages.
4. She could hide the fact from her family and get a surreptitious illegal abortion performed exposing herself to grave hazards. Methods of illegal abortion vary from the bizarre to the horrendous and are often lethal. Knitting needles, roots, twigs, catheters or harmful pastes

are introduced into the uterus in most unhygienic conditions leading to lacerations, bleeding, sepsis and death.

5. She could muster courage and risk the wrath of her parents and get an MTP performed by a qualified doctor under aseptic conditions in a well-equipped place. Unwed adolescents of the middle to higher income group have access to these facilities and usually do not suffer the complications of an abortion. Though free hospital facilities are available for the poor pregnant girls are wary of going there for fear of discovery.

Abortion per se, irrespective of the fact whether it is performed on an unmarried girl or a married matron with children, is not without risks. These include

Haemorrhage:

Sometimes the abortion is incompletely performed and the products of conception are retained in the uterine cavity. This leads to prolonged/intermittent bleeding, or bouts of profuse bleeding that can cause severe anemia, shock and death if the uterus is not evacuated in time.

Sepsis:

If the procedure is carried out with unsterile or improperly sterilised instruments, infection is introduced into the uterine cavity. In cases of incomplete abortion the retained necrotic (dead) bits of tissue can also get infected. Insertion of foreign bodies into the vagina like cotton wool, pastes, catheters can also lead to infection. The infection spreads to the adjoining organs resulting in pelvic inflammatory disease, which gives rise to chronic lower abdominal pain and general debility. If a virulent organism causes the infection and the body resistance is low it can result in septic shock syndrome and death.

Infertility:

Infection following septic abortion can lead to blockage of the fallopian tubes. This results in infertility, as the egg cannot be transplanted from the ovaries to the uterus on account of the blocked passage.

Injury of Genital Organs and Adjacent Structures:

Difficult abortions, abortions performed by inexperienced or untrained personnel can cause injuries to the uterus, bladder and intestines. If not diagnosed and operated upon in time the patient could bleed to death or die of sepsis later on. A badly mutilated uterus may have to be removed along with the intestines that have been injured or pulled out.

Oligomenorrhoea or Amenorrhoea:

Repeated MTPs lead to the thinning of the inner lining of the uterus. The opposing raw surfaces agglutinate leading to partial or complete obliteration of the uterine cavity. This results in scanty menstruation or complete cessation of periods. Sometimes the mouth of the uterus (cervix) gets blocked and the menstrual blood accumulates in the cavity leading to cramping pain at the time of menstruation. This has to be treated by dilating the cervical canal.

To these horrendous side effects are super-added problems peculiar to an unwed mother. These are

* Immense social, psychological and financial pressures and the need for total secrecy.

* An unmarried girl usually comes when the pregnancy is more advanced as compared to her married counterparts. It could be because she is genuinely unaware of the fact that she is pregnant (some young girls do not know that sexual intercourse leads to pregnancy) or she has irregular periods and discovers her pregnancy quite late. She may try to conceal her pregnancy as long as possible out fear social disgrace or indulges in wishful thinking, hoping against hope that she would have her periods in the next cycle. Once a pregnancy reaches 12 weeks and above the risks increase. At this stage the simpler method of suction evacuation is not possible and labour has to be induced either by injections, IV drips or intrauterine manipulations. All this leads to greater risks and hours of physical pain. The psychological scars may never heal. In case of complications the girl may become a chronic invalid or end up losing her life.

* If the above methods of inducing abortions fail operative interference has to be resorted to, which leave a permanent scar on the uterus. A scarred uterus needs special surveillance in subsequent pregnancies. After marriage, the girl may be able to explain away the abdominal scar but how is she to own up the presence of the uterine scar to her new family and their family doctor?

* Even suction evacuation, which is performed with ease in a woman who has borne children, is fraught with

difficulties in a first pregnancy. This is because the cervix (the mouth of the uterus) is so tightly closed than the force used in negotiating it may create a false passage or lead to the perforation of uterus. The latter may need an urgent operation to sew up the hole in the uterus.

* Another fact overlooked while performing an abortion in an unmarried girl is her blood group. Girls who are Rh negative need to take an expensive injection with 72 hours of the abortion so that subsequent babies, do not suffer the consequences of Rh iso-immunisation. For this she has neither the inclination nor the money.

It is high time that we accept the fact that with economic liberation, changing social, cultural and moral values more and more adolescent girls will be sexually active and pregnancy is a natural fall out of such activity. Instead of ignoring such an important issue or fuming in moral outrage society will be served best by taking a practical approach. A few guidelines listed below can help.

* Inculcate strong moral values in teenagers.

* Giving them a proper sex education at home and educational centres so that they can make an informed choice.

* They should be aware of the existence of an entity called 'Reproductive health', which needs as much looking after as physical, mental and psychological health.

* They should have access to reproductive information, counseling and free contraceptive services. They should

know that emergency contraceptives are available for isolated unplanned and therefore unprepared for sexual act.

* Once an unwed girl discovers that she has missed her period she should confirm or rule out a pregnancy by a simple Pregnancy Test Kit that is available across the counter at most chemist shops.

* Having confirmed that she is pregnant and there is no desire or possibility of an early marriage the sooner the MTP is performed the lesser will be the chances of complications. Risks, pain and expense increase with every advancing week. Experts under aseptic precautions in well-equipped centres should perform the MTP. Antibiotic cover will ensure against infection and its sequelae.

* It is wisest to confide in her parents. After the initial outburst they will hide her predicament from society and help her get a safe abortion. They will be around in case an emergency arises to give her the much-needed moral and financial support. Poor parents would do well to take their daughter for a MTP to a government hospital instead of an untrained Dai who might kill her.

* Her blood group should be tested and the appropriate injection given within 72 hours of the abortion in case she turns out to be Rh negative.

* As the risks of MTP are life threatening she should never go for such a procedure alone. If she escapes the physical complications there is a very real risk of blackmail by unscrupulous hospital staff.

Chapter-13
Adolescent Pregnancy

Despite the child marriage restrain act of 1978, the average age at which a girl gets married in rural India is 15 years. Even in urban government hospitals 30% of the women attending antenatal clinic are below the age of 18 years. Pregnancy and child bearing at such an early age adversely affects the physical, mental and social well being of the girl. Mentally the girl is not prepared to take on the responsibilities of motherhood. Her education is cut short, limiting opportunities for employment and income earning. This leaves her at the mercy of her husband and his family, further diminishing her sense of self worth. Besides the fatigue of repeated childbearing, nursing and rearing the girl had to tolerate sexual abuse and incessant work that is neither acknowledged nor rewarded. To cap it all she suffers from malnutrition, anemia and depleted calcium stores.

Pregnancy at such a tender age results in a high maternal and infant mortality rate. Besides the complications inherent in an adolescent pregnancy there are hardly any health care facilities available in far-flung villages. Antenatal care is unheard of. Complications such as poor fetal growth, high blood pressure, twins, and abnormal position of the baby, small pelvis are not detected during pregnancy leading to obstetric catastrophes. Avoidable fatalities due to maternal and fetal tetanus are rampant. Untrained dais deliver women with bare unclean hands causing sepsis and haemorrhage which are the leading causes of maternal death. In the case of an emergency, transportation is primitive and medical care miles away. It is not uncommon to see a pale, swollen comatose girl with an undelivered baby, convulsing all the way from their village to the city. Needless to say many of them die. Others come with obstructed labour (due to small pelvic bones) and ruptured uterus, retained placenta (afterbirth), profuse bleeding - emergencies that, had facilities been available, could have been managed and saved the life of the girl.

Complications like anemia, nutritional deficiencies begin during pregnancy and affect mother and fetus alike. Pregnancy induced high blood pressure occurs more commonly teenage pregnancies. The baby does not grow appropriately for his age resulting in low birth weight babies that fail to thrive. Premature births and intrauterine death of the baby is not an uncommon occurrence. Obstructed labour due to a small bony pelvis and immature outlet leads to higher rate of interference and operative delivery. If she survives the birth, haemorrhage and infection there is good chance that she may go into post delivery depression. Hardly out of childhood herself she is ill equipped rear a child. A suckling infant depletes her calcium reserves. Unaware of contraception, she conceives her second child far too soon which leads to further deterioration in her health.

If this is the state of a teenage girl pregnant with a legitimate child one can well imagine the plight of an unwed adolescent mother. Irregular periods, lack of knowledge as regards contraception, ignorance about the importance of a missed period lead to undesired conceptions. In many cases the pregnancy is hid out of fear or shame till it is advanced to a stage when abortion impossible. Per force the disgraced, ostracised girl has to deliver her illegitimate offspring. The raging father, the abusive mother, the absconding boyfriend, the family dishonour, the deep psychological distress add to her woes. Physical neglect, the lack of antenatal care and nutrition lead to poor obstetric performance.

With the increase in urbanisation, industrialisation and population the number of unwed teenage mother are on the rise in our country. A survey conducted in a general hospital on unmarried pregnant women over a period of two years revealed some startling facts.

* Of the 100 cases studied 76% of the girls were below 20 years of age.

* A majority of girls willfully gave their consent for sexual activity. The reasons given were curiosity, promise of marriage, receipt of gifts and persistence by their boyfriends. Only four cases were of rape, which were not reported due to fear of social discrimination. Two girls were involved in prostitution.

* About 40% were unaware of contraception, 60% were aware but did not use any protective measures while 10% used condoms but conceived in spite of them.
* Only one girl was admitted for attempted suicide while another, 'accidentally' slept over her newborn child killing it.
* Social and family history revealed that 30% of these girls came from a single parent family. History of marital discord, child abuse and alcoholism was present in about 40% of cases.
* Most of them reported late and had to undergo either a high-risk second trimester abortion or delivery.

Besides the obstetrics care by doctors, social workers were deputed to council the girl. They explored possibilities of her marrying the father of the unborn child, made arrangements for adoption of the baby and rehabilitation of the mother. If adoption of the baby was decided upon, maternal child bonding was not allowed to take place by keeping the two in separate rooms.

The stigma attached to a girl who had borne an illegitimate child pursues her throughout life. There occur psychological and behavioural problems that lead to marital and social maladjustment in later life. For many there is separation from their family, disruption in education, decreased earning capacity and indulgence in prostitution. Children born out of wedlock are discriminated against throughout life. There are increased psychosocial problems in such children and a high incidence of juvenile delinquency.

To decrease the incidence of adolescent sex, abortions and pregnancies they should be given a proper sex education. There should be a healthy interaction between the sexes. Schools and colleges should keep them totally involved in their education and careers so that they are not obsessed with sexual matters. They should be made to work for socially relevant causes like adult literacy, environment improvement etc. in their spare time. Debates, cultural activities, sports, art, literary events should be promoted in a big way so that the energies of the adolescent are diverted towards socially productive (and not reproductive) activities.

If unfortunately, a girl has succumbed her sexuality and is found to be pregnant do not reject her. She is to be cared for not condemned for she needs you more than ever at this vulnerable point of her life. She is frightened and a shamed and regrets her indulgence. Help her through the crisis so that she does not end up as a physical and emotional wreck. Parents and society alike should give her a second chance. There is still much that can be salvaged from her young life yet.

Part- 4

Chapter-14

Vaginal Discharge & Sexually Transmitted Diseases

Adolescent girls are very concerned with vaginal discharge. It could be physiological but it must be kept in mind that in those who are sexually active it may well be associated with sexually transmitted disease (STD). Physiological discharge is not malodorous. It varies in consistency and quantity in different phases of the menstrual cycle. It tends to be thick and white in the pre and postmenstrual phase and thin and transparent in mid-cycle around the time of ovulation. As the time of sexual excitement bartholin's glands situated at the vulval opening secrete a thin slimy discharge to lubricate the vagina.

Any discharge that is malodorous, discolored and/or associated with itching is due to infection and needs prompt treatment. Though the signs and symptoms of vaginal infections are similar in the adolescent and the adult, the former are at a greater risk on account of their ignorance. Most are unaware of the fact that unprotected sexual activity with an infected partner can cause harm. Once the symptoms appear early medical relief in not sought on account of embarrassment or inaccessibility of medical facilities. Also, it must be kept in mind that peri-pubertal girls are more prone to infection than her adult counterparts because the protective female hormone, oestrogen is relatively deficient.

Conditions that lead to vaginal discharge are:

* Poor personal hygiene.
* Worm infestation chiefly pinworms.
* Foreign bodies like diaphragm, condom, cotton balls, tampons etc. in the vagina.
* Cervical erosion - this is a condition when the inner lining of the uterus (including secretory glands) extends on to the cervix leading to redness and discharge.
* Oral contraceptives.
* Intrauterine contraceptive devices.
* Tight undergarments or underwear of synthetic material like nylon.
* Hormonal disturbances.
* Allergic and chemical reactions to certain deodorants, soaps and detergents used either as douches or on the external genitalia.
* Secondary to respiratory and urinary infections.
* Last but not the least of all STD.

The STD that lead to vaginal infection are

Candida

This is a fungal infection of the lower genital area characterised by intense itching and thick curdy white discharge. The local area is red and swollen and there is burning while urination. While a large proportion of people infected by candid remain symptom free they can infect their sex partners. Diabetics, pregnant women and those on oral contraceptive pills are more susceptible to candida infection. Recurrence rate is high.

Trichomonal Infection

This is characterised by the flow of a copious, foul smelling, frothy discharge of a yellowish green colour. It is accompanied by soreness of the external genitalia, pain during urination and intercourse.

Bacterial Vaginosis

There is characterised by the presence of a thin skimmed milk like discharge with a fishy odour. There are no signs of inflammation like soreness and swelling.

Gonorrhoea

Quite often gonorrhoea is asymtpomatic. Those that are overtly infected complain of difficulty in passing urine (dysuria) and pain in the lower abdomen. There is a purulent vaginal discharge; those indulging in anal sex have an inflamed rectum while oral sex with an infected partner results in swelling, redness and soreness of throat. An infected mother can pass the disease to her newborn form her vaginal passage leading to purulent discharge from the baby's eyes. If untreated, it can cause blindness.

Chlamydia

This is commonest sexually transmitted disease. It is prevalent chiefly amongst young promiscuous, unmarried females of the lower socio-economic strata. Presence of concomitant other STD is approximately 25%. Though the disease can permanently damage the upper genital system leading to infertility and chronic pelvic pain, it remains asymptomatic in as high as 70% of cases. Those that are symptomatic have a yellowish green vaginal discharge. They have urinary symptoms like dysuria and pus discharge though urine culture report is usually sterile. It can lead to preterm delivery and infect the newborn.

As the clinical signs and symptoms are rare and the long-term sequelae high, the condition has to be actively looked for and treated vigorously.

Other STD cause local lesions instead of vaginal discharge. These include

Syphilis

After an incubation period of about 3 weeks a single hard painless swelling appears in the genital region. Those indulging in extra- genital sex may have the lesions on the lips, mouth, nipples and anus. The 'chancre' as the lesion is called gradually erodes and ulcerates. The ulcer is painless, punched out with clean raised borders. As the chancre may appear deep in the vagina and as it is painless the female may be unaware of the fact that she has got syphilis. This may lead to the spread of infection to her sex partners and also delay in seeking treatment. The chancre heals of its own accord within a few weeks.

If untreated syphilis progresses to the secondary stage that is characterised by symmetrical bilateral skin rash particularly on the soles and palms. Condyloma - polypoid growths may appear in warm moist areas like the perineum - the area between the genitals and anus. These lesions are highly infective. After a latent period (when the disease is not infective) 30% patients progress to the tertiary stage that may involve the vascular and neurological systems. A mother can infect her unborn child at any stage. The chances of a stillbirth, neonatal death (death within 7 days of birth) occurring in a pregnant woman with syphilis is very high. At times a live baby is born with signs and symptoms of congenital syphilis.

Penicillin is the drug of choice in all stages of syphilis though other drugs have to be given to those patients sensitive to penicillin. Sexual activity can be resumed within 7-10 days of completion of therapy or once the lesions have completely healed.

Genital Herpes

This is a viral infection that occurs after genital or oro-genital sexual contact with an infected partner. Chances of infection are as high as 75%. The incubation period is 2-10 days. There may be fever and general malaise. Primary infection presents as painful lesions on the external genitalia that are either filled with clear fluid or pus. There is pain and dysuria. After some time this lesion burst leaving behind shallow painful ulcers that crust and heal in approximately 19 days.

Recurrent infection can take place within a period of 1-3 months and is usually triggered by mental stress, menstrual distress, intercourse and insomnia. Prior to the eruption of lesions there appears a feeling of tingling or itching on the area where the eruptions are likely to appear. This is a characteristic peculiar to secondary infection. Healing occurs within two weeks.

Genital herpes responds very well to an antiviral drug called acylovir. Special care has to be taken in a pregnant woman, as the infection is likely to spread to the newborn.

Human Papillomavirus

Human papilloma virus occurs predominantly in the age group between 15-30 years. The latent period is 3 months or even longer. It leads to the formation of genital warts. Of late, its connection with genital cancer has been proved beyond doubt. It is a difficult condition to treat and there is a high recurrence rate either due to an untreated partner or the presence of latent virus beneath a normal looking skin.

The virus has a predilection for adolescents perhaps due to the immaturity of the genital tract. A number of fleshy warts grow over the external genitalia extending up to the perineum and anus. They bleed easily in a pregnant woman and are difficult to control.

Treatment consists of local application of toxic drugs like podophyllin at weekly intervals. If unsuccessful, or if the woman is pregnant cryotherapy or laser ablation can be tried.

AIDS

The latest and scariest of all STD is vast enough to demand a larger canvas and is dealt with separately.

Treatment

The havoc wrought by sexually transmitted diseases on the genital system of a woman can make her a reproductive cripple for life. Hence it is imperative that the patient seeks medical advice as soon as she notices anything untoward. As soon as the diagnosis of STD is confirmed specific treatment should be started in the right dose for the appropriate period of time. It is mandatory that both sexual partners be treated irrespective of the fact that one of them has no complaints for the disease spreads in a ping-pong manner from one partner to the other.

Besides there are certain general guidelines that should be followed.

* Personal hygiene is of paramount importance.
* Worms if present should be eradicated.
* Foreign bodies impacted in the vagina should to be removed.
* Strong detergents and soaps that lead to allergic reaction are best avoided.
* Cervical erosion is treated by cryotherapy.
* Education regarding abstinence or safe sex with the use of barrier contraceptives is imperative though the above cannot prevent all STD.

* Girls suffering from sexual abuse have to be treated both physically and psychologically.
* Infection usually occurs in the immediate postmenstrual period when people are most lax about contraception as it is regarded as the 'safe period' and pregnancy is least likely to occur, so condoms should be used even in this period.

Chapter-15
AIDS & the Adolescent

AIDS is the scourge of modern times. It is a disease of young sexually active people and is spreading alarmingly in epidemic proportions. As there are no externally visible signs in the initial stage, as it takes years for the disease to develop into its full-fledged lethal form people do not realise the gravity of the situation. If not checked in time there will soon come a time when people in their prime will be demolished leaving behind a woeful world of helpless children and elders. It is important to know that though AIDS is preventable there is no cure available - as yet.

Adolescence represents a time of sexual experimentation and risk taking. This is manifested in the form of unprotected intercourse, multiple sex partners and homosexuality. AIDS was first discovered in homosexual males in the early eighties. Cigarettes, alcohol and substance abuse are rampant. Added to this is ignorance about the hazards of unprotected sex with an infected partner or the sharing of needles for drug injection. All this is an open invitation to the AIDS virus.

Not all adolescents are sex crazed drug addicts but what if a morally strong, socially well-adjusted virgin gets married to a normal looking person who is HIV positive? She will contract the dreaded disease through no fault of hers. Children conceived from such unions are doomed from the outset for the infection can be transmitted from the mother to her infant.

What is AIDS?

AIDS is an acronym for Acquired Immuno Deficiency Syndrome. It is caused by a retrovirus called Human Immuno-deficiency virus (HIV), which selectively infect and destroy a certain type of white blood cells called the CD_4 cells. As these are responsible for the immunological response of the body, decrease in their count leads to a failure of the defense mechanism of the body. Various opportunistic infective organisms invade the body, as it is unable to resist the onslaught. The patient eventually succumbs to these secondary infections.

How is AIDS acquired?

* Through homosexual or heterosexual contact.
* By sharing of needles with an infected person. Drug addicts are especially prone to such a mode of infection.
* Infected mothers can transmit the infection to their offspring, either in the womb or through breast milk.
* By transfusion of infected blood or blood products.
* Health workers can get accidentally inoculated with the virus by penetrating injuries or infected needles.

Though the HIV virus is secreted in small quantities in saliva, urine and tears it is unlikely that the disease spreads through these routes.

AIDS does not spread by insect bite or casual contact. People living with an HIV positive person or sharing the same work place do not catch the infection. In fact, the virus is so delicate that soap and water or household bleach can destroy it. The concentration of HIV virus is high in blood, blood products and body fluids. Care must be taken to avoid contact with these.

What is the course of the disease?

Once a person contracts the infection through any of the above means he/she may or may not suffer from a mild flu like symptoms or allergic skin conditions. These subside of their own accord after a while. It takes a period of 6-12 weeks for the patient to become sero-positive, which means that antibodies to the virus can be detected in the blood only after this period. This is called the 'window period' and the implications are grave for the person is quite capable of spreading the infection though his blood tests negative for HIV. Hence however diligently a blood sample is tested in a blood bank one cannot be sure if the donor is infected unless he is re-tested after a period of 12 weeks or so and has not indulged in high risk behaviour in the meantime.

Even after a person become sero-positive he may remain asymptomatic for years afterwards. Though there are no external manifestations of the disease the sero-positive individual can spread the infection by any of the means mentioned above.

What are the signs and symptoms of AIDS?

It takes an average of 8 years for a sero-positive case to develop into full-fledged case of AIDS. The signs and symptoms are:

* Unexplained weight loss.
* Chronic diarrhoea.
* Low-grade fever.
* Fatigue.
* Chronic cough.
* Skin problems

Any person who develops one or more of the above signs and symptoms should be tested for HIV virus. Any known HIV positive case that develops one or more of the above symptoms becomes a case of AIDS. By now the body resistance has considerably weakened and opportunistic infections invade the body. TB has returned in a big way on account of AIDS. Herpes, oral thrush (furry white growth in the mouth and food pipe due to the fungus candida), Kaposi's Sarcoma (a low grade, slow growing skin cancer) and a rare variety of intractable penumonia caused by penumocytis carnii infect the weakened body. The patient also suffers from breathlessness, visual impairment and neurological problems like meningitis and progressive dementia.

How is a case of AIDS diagnosed?

A highly sensitive Eliza test detects the presence of antibodies to HIV virus in the blood. Once Eliza has been found positive further confirmation is necessary by Western Blot method.

How is AIDS treated?

Treatment has to be instigated at 3 levels.

* Control of secondary infections.
* Control of the disease itself and
* Rebuilding of the body's defense mechanism.

Kaposi's Sarcoma is treated by chemotherapy, which further lowers the body's resistance. Appropriate drugs treat pneumonia and TB but the cure rate is low and recurrence rates high.

Expensive antiviral drugs are now available in the market that prolong the life span considerably but are beyond the reach of most Indians who have to per force give up treatment midway.

Increasing the body's resistance by bone marrow transplant has been tried without much success.

What can be done to prevent the occurrence of AIDS?

It is best not to indulge in high-risk behaviour. Abstinence is ideal for the unmarried and safe single partner sex for the married. If one's sexuality comes in the way of other day-to-day activities and marriage is yet a distant dream, masturbation is perhaps the only way one can find sexual relief and one need not feel guilty about it. Madness, impotency, infertility said to be the repercussions of such indulgence are pure myths and should be viewed as such. If the adolescent is sexually active, it is wise to use barrier methods of contraception. Sex workers should insist on the use of condoms by their clients. Condoms considerably reduce the risk of AIDS but they are not fool- proof.

Those on drugs should try their best to give up the habit. If that is not possible in the immediate future, sharing of needles should be stopped. Sterile disposable syringes and needles will reduce the risk of the evil of AIDS. Blood banks must test all prospective donors for AIDS.

HIV positive women of childbearing age should avoid getting pregnant for the chances of bringing an infected baby into the world are high. Those with early pregnancy should be given the option of abortion.

Newer antiviral drugs taken by the pregnant mother reduce the risk of vertical transmission to the infant. Health workers should take the mandatory protections against AIDS for blood and body fluids are highly infective. They should wear plastic disposable gowns, facemasks, specs and double gloves while conducting deliveries and operations. Care must be taken not to sustain inadvertent needle pricks. Hospital waste should be treated by household bleach and disposed according to prescribed norms. Needles and syringes should be destroyed before being discarded so that they are not re-used

If accidental exposure does occur, antiviral drugs started within 4 hrs. and taken for at least 4 weeks prevents AIDS infection. The foot-loose fancy-free teenager who thinks nothing of promiscuous sexual behavior and experimenting with drugs before settling down to matrimony and fidelity should understand that the perils of such activities are irreversible. Even is she is asymptomatic at the moment she may turn into a full-blown case of AIDS when she is a young matron with a child or two and is needed as never before. Her world will collapse around her like a pack of cards and there is nothing much she can do about it.

A person found to be HIV positive should not be treated as a social outcast. His family should not shun him for fear getting infected. Touching an HIV positive individual, living in the same house or breathing the same air with him does not acquire AIDS. Abroad, councilors have been marrying AIDS positive individuals to each other so that the remaining years are spent in companionship and not anguish. All the same, never has the adage 'Prevention is better than cure' been truer than in the case of AIDS.

Chapter-16

Pelvic Inflammatory Disease (PID) and Pelvic Tuberculosis

Pelvic inflammatory disease (PID) is a term given to infections of the upper genital organs - uterus, tubes and ovaries. It is usually an aftermath of sexually transmitted diseases (STD). Though it can occur in women at any time of their reproductive life, adolescence is a period of greatest risk. It requires aggressive treatment to prevent long-term sequelae like chronic pelvic pain and infertility.

Conditions that predispose a girl to PID are:

* Increasing incidence of sexual activity amongst adolescents. The motile sperms carry the infective organisms to the upper genital tract.
* Age - girls who have their first intercourse before the age of 15 are 4 times more likely to develop PID in contrast to those who first had sex after 18 years of age.
* Girls who had sex with five or more partners have a

higher tendency towards PID than those who have relation with only one partner.

* Poor personal hygiene.
* Excessive blood loss during periods.
* Low levels of protective antibodies in a young girl predispose her to infection and aid in rapid spread.
* Early marriage and childbirth.
* Tissue destruction after abortions or delivery, make the genital system particularly vulnerable to infective organisms.
* Other health risk behaviour like smoking, drugs and alcoholism are more commonly found in adolescents who acquire STD and PID.
* Use of intrauterine contraceptive device (IUCD)
* Douching.

Barrier contraceptives significantly reduce the incidence of STD & PID, but the knowledge regarding contraceptives is poor amongst adolescents. Those who have the knowledge, have limited access to such contraceptive measures.

Signs and symptoms of PID are:

* Increase in menstrual flow - this occurs in the initial phase, when the infection is restricted to the inner lining of the uterus.
* Pain lower abdomen - due to inflammation of the tubal wall. This may be unilateral or bilateral, depending on whether one or both tubes are involved.
* There may be fever, malaise, nausea and vomiting.

* Vaginal discharge.
* Dyspareunia (painful intercourse), which is often difficult to treat. This is due to the leakage of the inflammatory exudate from the tubes into the abdominal cavity leading to adhesions and painful mass formation.
* The tubes may get blocked, or damaged resulting in infertility as the ova cannot be transported from the ovaries to the uterus.
* Sometimes the fertilized ovum get lodged in the convoluted, diseased tube in place of the uterus, resulting in a potentially life threatening condition called ectopic pregnancy (pregnancy at a site other than the uterus). The tube ruptures, leading to intense pain, internal haemorrhage, shock and death.

The commonest infective organisms are

* *Gonococci* - is responsible for 15-18% of cases of PID. There may be a severe clinical picture with fever, pain and burning while passing urine and pus discharge from the vagina, though 1/3rd of adolescents with gonorrhoeal infection may be asymptomatic. The response to treatment is also dramatic. The earlier the disease is treated, the lesser are the chances of long term sequelae in the form of blocked tubes etc.

* *Chlamydia* is the causative organism in 40-60% of cases. It has a longer history and a milder clinical course. Though it may be asymptomatic in a large proportion of cases the sequelae left behind are devastating.

* *Anaerobic infection* leads to a severe form of PID with the formation of pus and painful masses.

The acute pain of PID can be mistaken for that of appendicitis, especially if restricted to the right side, or ectopic pregnancy. If the girl is a virgin or there is no history sexual activity in the recent past, ectopic pregnancy can be ruled out, though PID can sometimes occur due to the spread of infection through blood. High blood counts indicate infection, while a urine test positive for pregnancy points towards ectopic pregnancy. Ultrasound is a very useful aid in diagnosing or ruling out PID. Culture sensitivity of a swab taken from the upper vagina is helpful in finding the exact nature of infection.

Treatment

PID in the adolescent has to be treated aggressively. Hospitalisation is recommended strongly by most doctors. Untreated or inadequately treated PID can lead to intractable chronic pelvic pain, back pain, painful intercourse, pelvic abscess, infertility and ectopic pregnancy - in short total ruination of her reproductive health.

The right antibiotic, in the right dose for the right duration of time is the mainstay of treatment. Painkillers and anti-inflammatory drugs are useful adjuvants. If the symptoms are severe IV fluids and IV antibiotics are given. Surgery is indicated when there are pelvic masses or abscesses. Treatment of the sexual partner is essential to prevent recurrence.

Prevention of PID in a teenager:

* Sex education.
* Prevention of early marriage and child bearing.
* Easy access to condoms.
* Avoidance of criminal abortions and MTP.
* Avoid multiple partners.
* Abstinence if possible till marriage.

No discourse on PID can be complete without a mention of Pelvic Tuberculosis, especially in the Indian context though even abroad, the disease has returned with a vengeance due to the increasing scourge of AIDS. TB bacilli reach the genital tract from a primary source (chiefly TB lungs) by the blood stream. 5-15% of girls with TB lung with develop genital tuberculosis. As opposed to ascending spread of STD from the lower genital tract, this spreads in a retrograde manner from the tubes to the uterus leaving in its wake, pelvic masses, blocked tubes and destruction of the inner lining of the uterus.

Clinical presentations

* The girl may be absolutely asymptomatic even though her reproductive ability is irreversibly destroyed.
* She could suffer from an initial phase of excessive periods. This is followed by scanty periods that may stop altogether after a while.
* Anemia, weight loss, low-grade fever, loss of appetite and night sweats as in TB elsewhere.
* Chronic pelvic pain.

* Masses in the pelvis.
* Vaginal discharge.
* Infertility.

Though a major contributory factor towards infertility pelvic tuberculosis is difficult to diagnose. It should always be kept in mind when a married girl has scanty periods and is unable to conceive. Also a strong family history of TB in the family or a past history of treated/untreated TB lung should rouse a high index of suspicion. Tests include ultrasound, biopsy, laparoscopy and hysteroscopy.

Treatment

Besides bed rest and adequate nutrition, treatment with a full course of multi-drug anti-tubercular therapy for at least six to nine months is mandatory. It is important to counsel the patient adequately and impress upon her the need for such prolonged medication. In cases of poor compliance resistance develops to the first line of treatment and newer expensive drugs with greater side effects have to be given.

Regular follow-ups are necessary. Clinical and symptomatic improvements are looked for. Drugs may have to be changed in cases of side effects that make compliance difficult or if the expected improvement in her general condition does not occur. The patient also needs a lot of morale boosting and reassurance that her disease is curable provided she adheres to the prescribed regimen. Surgery is necessary in cases with pelvic masses, persistent pelvic pain and poor responders to medical treatment.

With the increasing incidence of HIV related TB it is mandatory to test the presence of TB in HIV positive patients and vice versa. TB in an HIV positive individual spreads faster and responds poorly to treatment.

Though adequate therapy eradicates the disease per se, fertility is not restored. This is because the blocked, damaged, adherent and dilated tubes cannot transport the ova from the ovaries to the uterus and the damaged uterine lining does not allow implantation even if expensive artificial reproductive methods are tried.

Chapter-17
Vaginal Tampons & Toxic Shock Syndrome

Vaginal tampons were introduced in the market in the eighties. They spelt ultimate liberty from the messiness of menstruation. The more highly absorbable the fibre of the tampon the more it was coveted till society woke up to the alarming fact that tampons could lead to a potentially fatal condition called Toxic Shock Syndrome (TSS). TSS also occurs due to certain surgical causes unrelated to menses but TSS in association with tampons and menstruation is totally avoidable. It is imperative that mortality from such a preventable cause be avoided at all costs.

An organism called S aureus causes TSS. Women between 15-34 years of age are most susceptible to TSS. The onset is during menses and a vaginal tampon is usually found in place; though it may also occur a day or two after menses. The patient presents with fever, headache, body ache, abdominal pain vomiting and loose motions. There is a sunburn-like appearance on the skin. The disease progresses rapidly and taking a serious turn with the fall of blood pressure, delirium and profound shock. If adequate and instant therapy is begun and the girl survives this phase the skin begins to peel off chiefly from the palms and soles and is completely cast off by the 10th - 14th day.

As soon as the condition is diagnosed the patient is hospitalised and the tampon removed. She is put on IV fluids, antibiotics and life saving drugs. Recurrence can occur in 1/3rd of the patients and a woman who survived TSS should not be allowed to use tampons.

Girls/women desirous of using tampons should be educated about the existence of this potentially fatal albeit rare entity. They should be aware of the signs and symptoms of fever, vomiting diarrhoea, pain abdomen and rash so that they can report to a doctor at the earliest. After the connection between high absorbency tampons and TSS was confirmed the former have been removed from the market reducing the incidence of TSS considerably. The high absorbency tampons absorbed not only water by magnesium from the body leading to conditions conducive to the release of toxins from bacteria already present in the genital tract. Considering the exposure to a potentially fatal hazard, even low absorbency tampons should be used intermittently, for the shortest possible periods and alternated with pads.

Part- 5

Chapter-18

Mental Health of the Adolescent

Adolescence is a period of mental turmoil. There are dramatic physical changes that evoke significant behavioural and emotional reactions. There are social pressures and sexual stirrings that have an immediate and long- term impact on the psyche of the growing girl. Opposing factors bombard the brain putting a lot of strain on her mind. Though a most youngsters overcome the upheavals of this period and adjust to the changing conditions, quite a few succumb to the tension and suffer from an array of mental diseases.

Stress - the disease of this millenium has spared neither child nor adolescent. The modern youth is subjected to tenfold more stress than his counterpart underwent a decade ago. Competitive exams, highflying jobs, the relentless race for goals not reachable by all; ambitious career pursuits, parental pressure, peer pressure and Western influence disturb the mental equilibrium of the adolescent.

The factors that affect the mental health of an adolescent girl are:

* Dependence-Independence Conflict

There is a tug of war between the desire for freedom and the need for dependency. Adolescents behave in an aggressive, argumentative manner to prove their independence. The defy parental authority and social norms by wearing atrocious dresses, sporting weird hair styles; staying out late, drinking and smoking. They are ashamed of their restrictive, moralistic and old-fashioned parents and tend to contradict their viewpoint at every step.

* Family Versus Peer Pressure

Teenagers spend more time with their friends than with their families. Girls are especially close to their same sex friends, sharing secrets and personal thoughts they would not dare disclose to their parents. They shift their emotional dependence from their parents to their peers. They are particular about conforming to the dress and moral code of their friends and pay no heed to objections raised by the family. Though peers act as models for immediate behavioral patterns most teenagers usually turn to their parents for long term planning of future oriented goals. Social environment, family support and peer emulation may act as protective or risk factors depending upon the social circle she moves in and the atmosphere at home.

*Sexuality

Girls tend to view sexual maturity with mixed feelings. Menstruation is welcomed as a landmark development that makes them a 'real woman' and is resented at the same time for the inconvenience, embarrassment and discomfort it causes. The attitude of the girl towards menstruation depends largely on the attitude of her mother. Girls who mature at the right age tend to fare best. Early maturation of the sexual organs takes place in short obese girls. Though these girls are popular with the boys their academic performance tends to suffer. Those who mature later are thinner and taller than their counterparts.

Breast development is scrutinised with avid interest, as it is an external proclamation of their sexuality. Too large or too small a breast size is a cause of intense concern. In fact the girl gets upset psychologically if any outward manifestation of her sexuality - be it height, weight, breast development, hair growth varies from the norm.

At this age girls begin to take special care over their appearance, make up, clothes and hair-do in order to make themselves attractive to members of the opposite sex. They are inordinately pleased when boys show an interest in them. More often than not the sexual tension so generated culminates in sexual interaction. Though intensely pleasurable premarital sex is hazardous to her physical and mental health. Besides the physical risks of sexual activity, sexual jealousy, violence or betrayal may result in psychological scars that may tilt the mental balance towards the negative.

* Career

This is also a crucial time for making a career

choice. Conflicts arise when parents try to force marriage and domesticity on a girl desirous of studying further. If they are willing to concede to higher studies her career choice may not tally with theirs leading to discord and mental anguish. If she gets admission in a distant place her parents may not be willing to let her go out of sight on account of the sexual liability which further worsens the situation. Others want her to get into staid comfortable professions like medicine and teaching while her interests lie in fine arts or modeling. If forced to concede to parental authority thwarted desire may lead to depression.

Unhealthy competition with peers, the strain of trying to live up to parental expectations cause stress that further disturbs her mental equilibrium. Prolonged professional courses in places away from home may have an adverse effect on her mental health. Loneliness, inability to adjust to new environments or make new friends, promiscuity due lack of restrictions and decreased fear of discovery in distant places also jeopardise her mental health.

What sort of mental disorders are likely to occur in the adolescent?

These are:

Depression

There is an alarming increase in depressive disorders in the adolescence as role delineation and expectations change dramatically at this age and she is unable to cope. Hormonal changes and stress inducing factors add to her woes. Girls with low self-esteem, pessimistic thinking, forced submissiveness, lack of control over life events and proneness to excessive worrying are more likely to go into depression. Traditional upbringing of Indian girls fosters these traits and thereby increases the risks of depression.

The depressed adolescent girl may present as a typical text book picture of a depressed patient or her depression may be reflected in poor academic performance, sexual promiscuity, truancy or running away from home.

Suicide

Increasing rates of adolescent suicides are a significant health concern and a major cause of death in this age group. Pre and post examination tension, contribute largely to mental disorders in the competitive world of today. Fear of parental anger, ridicule of peers, remorse and lack of support by family or society pushes the girl towards suicide. A broken love affair is another common cause of suicide.

Anorexia Nervosa

About 66% of female adolescents are preoccupied with their weight as compared to 15% of adolescent boys. Anorexia nervosa is mainly observed in girls between the age group of 15-24 years. It occurs in 1-2% of all adolescent girls. Most of them either resort to near starvation (anorexia nervosa) or bingeing alternating with induced vomiting (bulimia) because they feel that they are fat. With reed thin models and film stars as role models these impressionable girls try to emulate them. A vicious cycle that soon goes beyond their control is soon established. Extreme cases of anorexia nervosa may suffer from reduction in breast size and cessation of menstruation.

Asthenia

A feeling of weakness and fatigue is usually observed in girls of this period of transition. Besides actual tiredness these girls say that they feel ill, feel awful, that they have a headache or are unable to concentrate. Some may be dissatisfied with life or sad. All these varied feelings are lumped under the heading of 'weakness' and have to be probed further to confirm what is really ailing them.

Anxiety Disorders

These include social phobia, extreme shyness and anxiety over exams and results. Hysterical behaviour and obsessive-compulsive disorders are also common in adolescence.

Identity Disorder

Identity disorder occurs as a result of severe distress and inability to reconcile oneself to issues relating to career choice, future goals, friendship, loyalties, morality, and sexuality. It is not a mental condition per se but manifests as a part of mental problems like mood disorders, psychotic disorders and personality disorder states.

Schizophrenia

Schizophrenia or split personality is another disorder common at this age though its incidence is equal in both boys and girls.

How does an adolescent girl cope with stress?

There are two ways of dealing with a problem - either you face it head on or you evade it. Adolescents usually resort to the latter. They use avoident coping strategies like listening to music, sleeping or sports instead of trying to solve the problem directly or seeking help. Only 20% adolescents with mental problems seek the help of professionals. Due to this psychologist and psychiatrist are unable to access those who really need their help. Parents are reluctant to acknowledge the presence of psychiatric disorders in their child on account of the stigma attached and hence do not take them to the concerned specialists.

How should the problem of adolescent mental health be dealt with?

* Parents and teacher should be trained to understand the psychology of the adolescent.
* Sex education in middle school is a must.
* Group therapy sessions should be held so that the adolescents understand the physical and emotional changes they are going through.
* Teaching the adolescent healthy coping mechanisms.
* If needed, parents and adolescents should not shy away from seeking professional help. There is no stigma attached to such endeavour. On the other hand a mentally balanced future is ensured for their offspring, if the problem isacknowledged and help sought at the earliest.

Chapter-19
Crimes Against the Adolescent Girl

Ever since conception the female child is at a disadvantage in India. Female feticide is rampant in urban and rural areas, amidst the rich and poor alike. Despite stringent laws being passed against ultrasonic sex determination (performed for the express purpose of aborting the female fetus), it flourishes in a clandestine manner. There are lamentations and despair at the birth of a daughter while there is celebration and joy at the arrival of a son. Female infanticide in rampant in many parts of India, the methods ranging from burying the child alive to stuffing her nostrils with sand to feeding her the milk of poisonous plants!

If she is 'allowed' to her survive there are deliberate lapses in nurturing her. She is deprived of adequate nutrition, education and health care. She is made to feel guilty for belonging to the wrong sex while her brother is loved and pampered. Despite all this, most girls reach adolescence for biologically the female is the stronger sex. Discrimination continues unabated. Even as her body is deprived of adequate nourishment, her mind of adequate developmental opportunities her psyche is battered by the negative attitude towards her very existence. She is constantly reminded of the burden she is to the family (this when she toils relentlessly from dawn to dusk) of the dowry her father will have to amass to get rid of her. As if this is not enough, her burgeoning sexuality makes her vulnerable to a host of sexual crimes No wonder it has been aptly remarked that 'For girls Adolescence is a nightmare'!

The crimes commonly committed against an adolescent girl are:

* Child marriage
* Mock marriage
* Bigamous marriage
* Kidnapping
* Sale
* Illicit trafficking
* Sexual violence
* Incest
* Forced prostitution as devdasis etc.
* Criminal abortion
* Cruelty.
* Acid throwing
* Wrongful confinement.
* Homicide including dowry deaths.

Of all these crimes, sexual violation is the most heinous. The girl often knows the culprit. Someone she trusts like her father, brother, uncle cousin or neighbour. The violation of her body and her trust and has far-reaching physical and psychological consequences.

Sexual violation occur in the form of

* Molestation when the actual act does not take place but other forms of sexual harassment is resorted to.
* Rape when intercourse occurs using force or threat of force. Sexual intercourse with a minor even with her consent amounts to statutory rape. In cases of incest the act is committed again and again on the helpless girl usually by a person she has to remain in continual proximity. Usually the perpetrator of crime has been sexually abused himself in childhood.
* Sexual perversion like exhibitionism when a man resorts to indecent exposure in front of the members of the opposite sex and pedophilia when a grown up man has sex with a minor of either sex. Some girls are subjected to unnatural sex acts like sodomy and lesbianism.

Most cases of rape and incest go unreported on account of the shame and stigma attached. Besides the physical trauma the girl suffers from mental trauma similar to that, which occurs after disasters like war and earthquakes. This is called rape trauma syndrome. The stress reaction to rape can be divided into two phases:

* Acute phase, which again can be overt - when the symptoms of stress are manifested in the form of fear, weeping, tenseness and restlessness. It could be controlled - when the girl's true feelings are masked or

subdued. She may develop headaches, fatigue, sleep-disturbances and urinary/bowel complaints. Emotional disturbances present as anger, humiliation and self-blame.

* The second phase, when the girl tries to come to terms with the situation but has nightmares, phobias and sex related problems later in life.

If the girl and her parents are reluctant to go to the police for fear of disgrace and ruination of future marital prospects, it is wise to consult a doctor so that physical wounds are repaired and prophylactic antibiotics are given against sexually transmitted diseases. Hormones can be given to prevent pregnancy. If the girl comes after she has missed her period the pregnancy should be terminated. She is called after 6 weeks and 12 weeks to be tested for HIV infection. Alternatively, she can be put on a 4 weeks antiviral therapy to minimize the risk of AIDS.

The more trusted her assailant the greater is the mental trauma. She should be given psychiatric help to overcome her psychological trauma and help her recover from the aftermath of sexual abuse.

Rape has far reaching effects on family life especially if the girl is married. 50% of married rape victims are divorced within a year of the offense.

Sexual intercourse with one's own wife if she is less than 15 years legally amounts to rape. This is rampant in areas in India where a child marriage is the custom despite the laws passed against it.

Enticing minor girls with the promise of marriage, arranging mock marriages or keeping her as the second wife, are but ploys to obtain her consent for sexual activity. Quite often these girls (who have run away from home under the romantic influence of these crooks) are left in the lurch. Some of them become pregnant and resort to criminal abortions or suicide. Others are kidnapped, sold to brothels and forced into the flesh trade. Girls are offered as Devdasis to the goddess Yellama and end up appeasing the sexual desire of men. In certain places girls are auctioned like cattle.

Those who refuse to give in to men/boys obsessed by them incur their wrath, which may manifest as acid throwing! This leads to permanent facial disfiguration and psychological hurt. Sexual jealousy may even lead to physical injury and killing of the girl who rejects the advances of unsuitable men.

Considering the fact that predators are lurking at every corner to violate the innocence of the girl child/adolescent they should be taught the difference between a good touch and a bad touch as soon as they are old enough to understand. They must confide in their mothers any untoward behavior by any male member of the family or outside. They should be made emotionally strong enough not be allured by romantic trappings and give in sexually to any man who can later exploit them. They should never give in to boyfriends who try to blackmail them into consenting for sex 'to prove her love for him' for the consequences are hazardous.

Chaper-20
Substance Abuse in the Adolescent

Substance abuse has become an international crisis. Tragically, like AIDS it destroys people in the prime of their lives. It cuts across neither all sections of society sparing neither gender nor age of the individual. Rich and poor alike, fall prey to its deadly allure. Alarmingly most cases of substance abuse begin in adolescence.

Though boys outnumber girls, an increasing majority of females are getting addicted to drugs. Prejudice against girls taking drugs is greater than men as they are groomed to become caretakers of the family and society and a deviant lifestyle could lead to disruption in expected gender roles.

The profile of the adolescent prone to substance abuse is one who is rebellious and indulges in aggressive behaviour. He/she is an academic underachiever and socially maladjusted. There is a feeling of isolation, alienation and neglect. Nuclear families, working parents, martial discord, broken homes further lead the adolescent down the path of self-destruction - especially if his peers are drug abusers. The above traits are common to adolescents of both sexes. Girls most likely to succumb to substance abuse are:

The Innocent Type

This type of girl is passive, docile, isolated and lonely. She has a poor self-esteem and is morally weak. Quite often a male on whom she is dependent upon introduces her to the habit. All too soon she becomes helpless to resist the power of the man and the drug(s) he supplies.

The Bohemian Type

The girl is usually forward, sexually active, free, irresponsible, morally condemned and out to have a good time.

The new generation girl

Young girls doing the popular dance/club scene, taking cue from their partners, consider cigarettes, alcohol and drugs as recreational past times - a good way any to wrap up a night out.

Curiosity goads youngsters to 'see what it is like'. They give drugs a try thinking that they are in control and can opt out whenever they feel like. To their dismay they realize soon enough that it is the drug that has taken control of them.

The stages they go through are:

Experimenting to discover effect.

↓

Soon they require the drug to seek effect.

↓

This is followed by repeated use.

↓

Habituation

↓

Drug Tolerance - when greater dose is required for the same effect.

↓

Drug Dependence - when the person cannot do without the drug.

↓

Withdrawal symptoms - when the effect of the drug wanes.

Besides the health risks due to drug abuse per se there are also the risks (due to needle sharing) of AIDS and hepatitis B. The substance abuser resorts to theft, prostitution, drug peddling and other criminal activities to obtain money for the drug their bodies crave. In the case of women, besides the above, drugs affect her mental health, her genitourinary system, reproductive capacity and the health of her baby.

The stepping-stones on the path of destruction are:

Cigarettes

↓

Beer or wine

↓

Hard liquor

↓

Marijuana

↓

Other illicit drugs like cocaine, heroin

↓

Multiple drug abuse

Recovery when it occurs is in the reverse order.

Drugs commonly abused are:

Cocaine

Street names are coke, snow and stardust. It is a central nervous system stimulant and is derived from cocoa plant. It is available in the form of an odourless white flaky powder that can be sniffed, injected or inhaled as fumes after being heated.

Highs:

Heightened alertness, euphoria, and reduced appetite.

Lows:

The effect lasts for 30-40 minutes after which there is a comedown characterised by anxiety, paranoia, depression and insomnia. Physical and psychological tolerance builds up rapidly. The person develops tremors, muscle twitching, cold sweats, and nausea; increase pulse and BP and mood changes.

Long-term effects:

Include nervousness, excitability, mood swings and bronchitis. There is loss of appetite, sleep and potency and a feeling of prosecution. Sharing of needles can lead to AIDS and Hepatitis B.

Effect on women:

Cocaine promises weight loss and increased energy levels, which may seem attractive to women. Most are unaware of the fact that it can also cause shorter and scantier periods and finally complete cessation of menstruation. Those with history of urinary tract infections are prone to recurrence on account of the dehydration. If pregnant it can lead to bleeding as a result of placental separation, abortion, premature labour or stillbirth.

Crack

This is a very expensive, chemically altered form of cocaine. It is either smoked or inhaled as fumes.

Highs:

There is an intense high of about 10-15 minutes.

Lows:

This is followed by a comedown 'crash' leading to depression, tiredness, irritability and panic. It is habit-forming as tolerance develops quickly.

Long-term effects:

Tolerance, dependency, paranoia, mood swings and feeling of prosecution. Health risks are grave and include cardiac arrest, bronchitis and dehydration.

Effect on women:

Are same as in cocaine.

Both cocaine and crack can be detected in urine up to 3 days of last consumption.

Heroin

Street name smack, brown, china white. White or light brown powder that can be eaten, swallowed, smoked or injected.

Highs:

Creates feeling of relaxation and warmth, relief from physical and mental pain.

Lows:

Withdrawal symptoms occur 8-12 hours after last dose and are characterised by sweating, nervousness and insomnia.

Long-term effects:

Include tolerance, dependency, constipation, decreased sex drive, unstable moods and hazards of needle use. Getting rid of heroin addiction is difficult as it can lead to diarrhoea, vomiting, insomnia, and hot and cold cramps.

Effects on women:

Heroin leads to decrease in fertility. Complications are rare. Babies get addicted in the uterus and have to withdraw under medical supervision. Regular use leads to erratic periods and cessation of menstruation altogether.

Heroin can be detected in urine 1-2 days after last use.

Cannabis (Marijuana)

Street names include ganja, hashish, pot and grass. It is usually smoked as a joint but can be eaten or brewed in tea.

Highs:

Enhanced sense of well being relaxed, talkative, happy, giggly and social with heightened senses.

Lows:

Thirst, hunger, reduced concentration and impaired memory. Paranoia, anxiety, nausea if taken along with alcohol or smoked with tobacco.

Long-term effects:

Lethargy, laziness and short term memory loss. As no filter is used while smoking it leads to a high incidence of lung cancer and cardiac disease.

Effect on women:

It has no specific effect on women.

Can be detected in urine 2-7 days after moderate use and up to 30 days after heavy use.

Ecstasy

Street names include love, Dennis the menace, dove, rolling stones, snowballs etc. Usually come in coloured tablet form or capsules, occasionally as powder.

Highs:

Suppresses pain, leading to a sense of well being and euphoria.

Lows:

The body temperature mechanism goes awry leading to dehydration, heat stroke, weight loss, fatigue, anxiety and depression. Death can occur if the heat stroke and dehydration are not managed actively.

Long-term effects:

Risk of brain damage that can trigger mental illness, epilepsy. Kidney and liver damage can occur leading to hepatitis and jaundice.

Effects on women:

Weight loss, menstrual upsets and urinary tract infection. Affects chances of conception. Can also affect the fetus.

LSD

Street names - acid, trips, tabs. Available as tablets, capsules, cubes, pellet or small squares of blotting paper with cartoons on them.

Short-term effects:

Start 30 minutes after use and last up to 12 hours. Causes hallucinations - changes colours, shapes and sizes. Causes increased salivation and nausea.

If in a good mood before taking the drug - good trip. If in a bad mood you get a terrifying nightmarish trip. Once you start a trip you cannot stop it even if it is frightening.

Long-term effect:

Not physically addictive but psychological upsets occur in those who have had a bad trip and have pre-existing mental problems. The mind can be permanently damaged. Flashbacks of the original trip can recur days, months even years after the original trip. Hazardous behaviour including suicide can occur.

Effects on women:

Not significant but best avoided in pregnancy.

Prevention & Treatment of Drug Abuse

Children should be taught about the hazards of substance abuse through interactive sessions at home and school. They could also be shown video clippings depicting the horrors of drug addiction as visual impact leaves lasting impressions. They should be made emotionally strong enough to resist the temptation to experiment with drugs.

Drug Mafia that has a sizable profit to make from the sales of addictive drugs is not above initiating children of elementary school into the vice. Schools should be particularly vigilant about sweet-sellers outside their schools that feed small amounts of drugs to innocent children without their knowledge so that they become addicted. Edibles should be only bought from the canteen within the campus, where the food can be tested from time to time.

Adolescents susceptible to substance abuse must be identified and given psychiatric help. Victims of familial neglect, broken homes, marital discord should be taken in hand either by their parents/extended family or the social worker/psychologist in school before it is too late. They should be helped to overcome their feeling of isolation, neglect and poor self-esteem. Aggression and rebellious behaviour may be attention-seeking devices. Instead of scolding and punishments give them the care and warmth they crave. Most drug abusers have peers who are already drug users/peddlers and indulge in other forms of promiscuous behaviour. Therefore parents should be vigilant about their children's whereabouts and the type of company they keep. Erratic irritable behavior should not be overlooked or ignored by lumping it under the convenient heading of adolescent blues. Tremors, muscular twitching should be viewed with grave concern.

To obtain money for a regular supply of drug the adolescents resort to theft, even from their own house and prostitution. Scare tactics are usually counter-productive. It is best to mobilise youth for youth. A sustained effort is needed. De-addiction centres offer admission and detoxification followed by after-treatment care and support. Some offer home visits too later on. Treatment should be done in the context of the family for emotional support is essential in helping the frightened adolescent to recover. Evoking feelings of guilt or indulging in lamentation and blame by the parents will serve no useful purpose at this stage. As detoxification is a difficult uphill process, the adolescent needs all the love and care, assurance and reassurance and support his family can give. After recovery care should be taken that there are no temptations and relapses.

An adolescent hooked on drugs should be aware of certain harm reduction information. He/she should be mindful of the hazards of using interchangeable needles for injection. This can lead to AIDS, hepatitis B, abscess formation, septicemia, pneumonia, gangrene, blood clotting defects and skin infection. Till the time he is motivated enough to want to get rid of the habit he should take the drug by routes other than injections or with the use of disposable needles. Needle exchanges services are available abroad with drug agencies and chemists. They give disposable needles, syringes and swabs in exchange of the used ones. Condoms are also distributed free.

In case of an emergency it is best is to take the victim to the hospital and come out clean with the treating staff so that necessary therapy can be initiated at once and a life saved. Hiding the fact that the patient is a substance abuser will lead to the wastage of precious time in arriving at a diagnosis.

If medical aid is not immediately available and a person has collapsed due to dehydration as a result of drug intake, cool him under a fan. Cold water with a bit of salt should be sipped - one pint in one hour - and not gulped down. Isotonic fluids are helpful to replace lost nutrients. Sweating is a good sign. Once the temperature comes down to normal wrap the patient in a blanket.

If the patient is a girl pregnancy should be confirmed or ruled out. Though drugs delay menstrual cycles it does not mean that pregnancy is impossible. Most women are unaware of this and take unnecessary risks. Even those who are aware of the fact lose their normal inhibitions when on drugs and contraceptive lapses result in pregnancy. Drugs, drink, smoking, promiscuous sexual behaviour often co-exist, jeopardising the chances of the baby in the womb. Street drugs are often cut with harmful things, which have to be eliminated by a liver and kidney already strained by the pregnancy. If the baby does not abort or die in the uterus it may be delivered prematurely or have a low birth weight or suffer from withdrawal symptoms. As the drug is secreted in the milk breast-feeding is contraindicated though doctors have recently found that if the mother's drug abuse is stable breast milk can reduce withdrawal symptoms in the newborn. Some hospitals offer postnatal services at home so that the care is consistent and on going. Counseling and self-help groups are important factors in preventing relapse when the girl returns to her home.

Prostitutes form a major chunk of women who abuse drugs. On the other hand a girl may begin to walk the streets to finance her drug use. They are reluctant to come to a hospital for fear of stigma and exposure. Lesbian drug users also suffer from the same inhibitions on account of their deviant life style and do not seek treatment. Certain NGOs employ people to reach out to females such as these who wouldn't normally access health care providers.

